Catholic Bible Study

The Gospel
of Luke

by

Father Joseph L. Ponessa, S.S.D.

and

Laurie Watson Manhardt, Ph.D.

Emmaus Road Publishing
1468 Parkview Circle
Steubenville, OH 43952

All rights reserved. Published in 2015
Printed in the United States of America

Library of Congress Control Number: 2015942317
ISBN: 978-1-941447-25-3

Cover design and layout by
Jacinta Calcut, Image Graphics & Design, www.image–gd.com

Cover artwork:
Antonio Allegri da Correggio (1526), *The Adoration of the Child*

Nihil obstat: Reverend Jose Valliparambil, STD, *Censor Deputatis*

Imprimatur: Most Reverend Michael William Warfel, DD
Bishop of Great Falls—Billings
May 1, 2015

The *nihil obstat* and *imprimatur* are official declarations that a work is considered to
be free from doctrinal or moral error. It is not implied that those who have granted the
same agree with the content, opinions, or statements expressed.

For additional information on the "Come and See~ Catholic Bible Study"
series visit www.CatholicBibleStudy.net

Catholic Bible Study

The Gospel of Luke

Introduction

But Mary kept all these things,
pondering them in her heart.
Luke 2:19

The Gospel according to Luke—Saint Irenaeus (AD 130–200), Tertullian (AD 160–222), Origen (AD 185–254), Eusebius (AD 260–340), and Saint Jerome (AD 342–420) all credit the authorship of the third Gospel and its sequel, the Acts of the Apostles, to the Greek-speaking physician Luke. A Syrian of Antioch, Luke was born a pagan, but later converted to Christianity. The Bible reveals that Luke accompanied Paul on some missionary journeys. Paul speaks of Luke three times in his New Testament letters. *Luke the beloved physician and Demas greet you* (Colossians 4:14). *Luke alone is with me* (2 Timothy 4:11). *Epaphras, my fellow prisoner in Christ Jesus, sends greetings to you, and so do Mark, Aristarchus, Demas, and Luke, my fellow workers* (Philemon 1:23–24).

The Gospel of Luke begins and ends in the temple. The ministry of Jesus begins and ends with prayer. In the beginning, Luke recalls the Old Testament prophecies and God's promises to Abraham and his posterity forever. At the end of the Gospel, when the Savior Jesus of Nazareth redeems the world from sin in His crucifixion and rises from the dead, God's promises and the Old Testament prophecies are fulfilled.

The Blessed Trinity emerges clearly in Luke's Gospel. God the Father speaks at the Baptism of Jesus in the Jordan River (Luke 3:22), and again at the Transfiguration (Luke 9:28–36). Jesus thanks the Father (Luke 10:21), and teaches His disciples when they pray to begin by addressing God as Father: *"Father, hallowed be your name"* (Luke 11:2). Jesus promises that the Father will give the Holy Spirit to those who ask Him (Luke 11:13). Jesus illustrates the lavish mercy and unconditional love of God the Father in telling the parable of the Prodigal Son (Luke 15:11ff). And, at the end of His Passion, while Jesus is dying on the Cross for the sins of the world, He says: *"Father, into your hands I commit my spirit"* (Luke 23:46).

Luke highlights Jesus' humanity by revealing His poor, humble birth, being placed in a manger in swaddling clothes. Jesus, tempted by the devil, shows temptation as the common experience of all people. Jesus visits friends, Martha and Mary, invites Himself to stay at Zacchaeus' house (Luke 19:5ff), and enjoys meals with people (Luke 22:8ff; 24:41). Jesus' divinity is manifested in the angel's announcement of His miraculous birth to the Virgin Mary by the power of the Holy Spirit. *"The Holy Spirit will come upon you, and the power of the Most High will overshadow you; therefore the child to be born will be called holy, the Son of God"* (Luke 1:35). God the Father confirms the divinity of Jesus at His baptism. The Holy Spirit descends upon Jesus in the form of a dove, *and a voice came from heaven, "You are my beloved Son; with you I am well pleased"* (Luke 3:22). If any doubt remains about the true identity of Jesus, the Transfiguration of Our Lord further enlightens it. While Jesus prays, His countenance is altered, His clothing becomes dazzling white, a cloud overshadows Him, *and a voice came out of the cloud, saying, "This is my Son, my Chosen; listen to him"* (Luke 9:35). Luke clearly reveals Jesus as true God and true man, the Second Person of the Blessed Trinity.

The Holy Spirit is referenced more than a dozen times in the Gospel of Luke. In the first four chapters of Luke alone, the Holy Spirit emerges nine times (Luke 1:15, 35, 41, 67; 2:25, 26; 3:16, 22; 4:1). Jesus *rejoiced in the Holy Spirit* (Luke 10:21). He warns that *"he who blasphemes against the Holy Spirit will not be forgiven"* (Luke 12:10), but promises that God the Father will send the Holy Spirit to those who ask (Luke 11:13). And, when His disciples are in trouble, they need not fear, *"for the Holy Spirit will teach you in that very hour what you ought to say"* (Luke 12:12).

Like Saul of Tarsus, Luke enjoyed a privileged liberal education, enabling him to write in elegant Greek. He writes primarily for a Gentile audience. Luke had other Gospels available to him. He researched, compared, and sought out primary sources to interview, like the Blessed Virgin Mother. Who else but Mary could have recounted these events?

+ Precise words of the Archangel Gabriel at the Annunciation (Luke 1:26–37);
+ Mary's visit to her elderly, pregnant, kinswoman Elizabeth (Luke 1:39–56);
+ The Nativity—where Mary gives birth to Jesus in a manger (Luke 2:1–7);
+ Visits from the shepherds to the Holy Family (Luke 2:8–20);
+ The Presentation of Jesus in the Temple (Luke 2:22–24);
+ Simeon's canticle and prophecy of suffering (Luke 2:25–35);
+ Prophetess Anna's thanksgiving (Luke 2:36–38);
+ Jesus, Mary, and Joseph's return to Nazareth (Luke 2:39–40);
+ The Finding of Jesus in the Temple (Luke 2:41–51).

All of the Joyful Mysteries of the Rosary can be found in the first two chapters of Luke. Most of what we learn and cherish about the infancy and childhood of Jesus comes from Luke, probably through his research and interviews with the Blessed Mother Mary.

Prayer features prominently in the Gospel of Luke. Formal prayers of the Church, which are recited every day in homes, convents, and monasteries around the world, originate in Luke. The Canticle of Zechariah, or *Benedictus* (Luke 1:68–79), is recited in the morning prayer of the Divine Office or Liturgy of the Hours. The Canticle of Mary, the *Magnificat* (Luke 1:46–55), provides the Gospel Canticle said in evening prayer. Simeon's Canticle, the *Nunc Dimittis* (Luke 2:29–32), closes night prayer. These prayers, often chanted or sung, provide a framework for the prayer of the Church. Jesus seeks out a lonely place to pray (Luke 4:42), and draws apart to pray before calling His disciples (Luke 6:12). He teaches us how to pray and encourages us to persevere in prayer (Luke 11:1ff).

Joy permeates the Gospel of Luke. From the joyous beginning when an angel of the Lord appears in the temple and announces the birth of John the Baptist to an elderly, childless couple, to the angel bringing news of great joy of the birth of the Savior to the shepherds in the fields, to the joy of the disciples on the road to Emmaus, whose hearts burned with unbelievable joy as Jesus explained the Scriptures to them, walked with them, and ate with them, Luke presents joy, joy, joy.

Luke also reveals Jesus' compassion for the poor. Mary and Joseph present Jesus in the temple and provide birds, which was the common offering of the poor. Jesus says, *"Blessed are you poor, for yours is the kingdom of God"* (Luke 6:20), and tells a parable about a rich man in Hades and the poor man, Lazarus, who was ignored (Luke 16:19ff). He recognizes the widow's mite (Luke 21:1–4) and commends her sacrificial generosity and trust in God.

One of the most interesting features of the Gospel of Luke involves his treatment of women. Women in the first century held little significance. Only a man would be accepted as a credible witness to testify in a trial. Widows and unmarried women were at the mercy of relatives for their very survival. Historians recount that when a baby boy was born, there would be rejoicing and great festivities. But, if the baby was a girl, the mourners were summoned to wail. Consider the amazing number of positive references involving women provided in the Gospel of Luke.

✟	Luke 1:24–25	Elizabeth conceives in her old age, and praises God.
✟	Luke 1:26–38	The Annunciation of God's invitation is presented to the Blessed Virgin Mary by the Archangel Gabriel.
✟	Luke 1:39–45	Mary visits Elizabeth, who calls Mary *"Blessed among women."*
✟	Luke 1:57–61	Elizabeth gives birth to John and names him as the angel directed.
✟	Luke 2:1ff	Mary gives birth to Jesus in Bethlehem.
✟	Luke 2:36	Prophetess Anna gives thanks to God for His redemption.
✟	Luke 2:41ff	Mary questions Jesus when He stays behind to teach in the temple.
✟	Luke 7:11–15	In Nain, Jesus raises a grieving widow's only son from death.
✟	Luke 7:36ff	Jesus shows mercy and forgives a sinful woman.
✟	Luke 8:1–3	Mary Magdalene, Joanna, and Susanna follow Jesus.
✟	Luke 8:40ff	Jesus heals Jairus' daughter and a hemorrhaging woman.
✟	Luke 10:38ff	Jesus visits Martha and Mary.
✟	Luke 13:10ff	Jesus heals a crippled woman.
✟	Luke 18:1–8	Jesus praises the persistence of a widow.
✟	Luke 23:27	Women bewail and lament the suffering of Jesus.
✟	Luke 23:28	Jesus speaks to the daughters of Jerusalem.
✟	Luke 23:55ff	Women follow the dead body of Jesus to the tomb.
✟	Luke 24:1–3	Women go to the tomb with spices to anoint Jesus' body.
✟	Luke 24:4–7	Men in dazzling appearance speak to the women at the tomb.
✟	Luke 24:8–10	Mary Magdalene, Joanna, Mary, and other women tell the Apostles the good news concerning the empty tomb.

Women feature prominently and positively in the Gospel of Luke. There are more references to women in Luke's Gospel than almost any other book of the Bible. Luke provides more information about Elizabeth and Mary than the other evangelists. Jesus interacts with women, and shows compassion even to a notoriously sinful woman. Luke reports these encounters in significant detail.

The Gospel of Luke may be very familiar to you. You have probably heard the Nativity story every Christmas since your childhood. Most people, even non-Christians, recognize the parable of the Prodigal Son. If possible, you might want to take a retreat day and read the entire fifty-two chapters of Luke's Gospel and his Acts of the Apostles at one time. You could also pray to the Holy Spirit that you might receive fresh insights and gain a more profound appreciation of the mysteries of God as you study. May God surprise you with joy as you study and delve deeper into the Gospel of Luke. Remember, God always has more to offer than you can expect or imagine. God is good!

What You Need

To do this Bible Study, you will need a Catholic Bible and the Catechism of the Catholic Church (CCC). The Catechism is available in most bookstores, and it can be accessed on the Internet at http://www.vatican.va/archive/ENG0015/_INDEX.HTM or at http://www.usccb.org/beliefs-and-teachings/what-we-believe/catechism/catechism-of-the-catholic-church/.

In choosing a Bible, remember that the Catholic Bible contains seventy-three books. If you find Sirach and Tobit in your Bible's table of contents, you have a complete Catholic Bible. The Council of Hippo approved these seventy-three books in AD 393, and this has remained the official canon of Sacred Scripture since the fourth century. The Council of Trent in AD 1546 reaffirmed these divinely inspired books as the canon of the Bible.

For Bible study purposes, choose a word-for-word, literal translation rather than a paraphrase. An excellent English translation is the Revised Standard Version Catholic Edition (RSVCE) Bible. **Because of different verse numbering in these Bibles, the RSVCE second edition by Ignatius Press will be the easiest to consult to complete the home study questions in the *Come and See ~ Catholic Bible Study* series.**

How To Do This Bible Study

1. Pray to the Holy Spirit to enlighten your mind and spirit.
2. Read the Bible passages for the first chapter.
3. Read the commentary in this book.
4. Use your Bible and Catechism to write answers to the home study questions.
5. Watch the videotape lecture that goes with this study.
6. In a small group, share your answers aloud on those questions.
7. End with a short prayer.

Practical Considerations

+ Ask God for wisdom about whom to study with, where, and when to meet.
+ Gather a small prayer group to pray for your Bible study and your specific needs.
+ Show this book to your pastor and obtain his approval and direction.
+ Find an appropriate location. Start in someone's home or in the parish hall if the space is available and the pastor will allow it.
+ Hire a babysitter for mothers with young children and share the cost amongst everyone, find some volunteers to provide childcare, or form a co-op to teach children.

Pray that God will anoint specific people to lead your study. Faithful, practicing Catholics are needed to fill the following positions:

+ **Teachers**—Pray, read commentaries, and prepare a short wrap-up lecture.
+ **Prayer Leaders**—Open Bible study with a short prayer.
+ **Children's Teachers**—Teach the young children who come to Bible study.
+ **Coordinators**—Communicate with parish personnel about needs for rooms, microphones, and video equipment. Make sure rooms are left in good shape.
+ **Small Group Facilitators** will be needed for each small group. Try to enlist two mature Catholics who are good listeners to serve together as co-leaders to:

  ≈ Make a nametag for each member of the small group and pray for them every day.
  ≈ Meet before the study to pray with other leaders.
  ≈ Discuss all the questions in the lesson each week. Begin and end on time.
  ≈ Make sure that each person in the group shares each week.
  ≈ Make sure that no one person dominates the discussion, including you!
  ≈ Keep the discussion positive and focused on the week's lesson.
  ≈ Speak kindly and charitably. Avoid any negative or uncharitable speech.
  ≈ Listen well! Keep your ears open and your eyes on the person speaking.
  ≈ Give your full attention to the person speaking. Be comfortable with silence.
  ≈ If questions, misunderstandings, or disagreements arise, refer them to the question box for a teacher to research or the parish priest to answer later.
  ≈ Arrange for a social activity each month.

More Practical Considerations

+ Twelve to fifteen people make the best size for small groups. When you get too many people in a group, break into two smaller groups.
+ Sit next to the most talkative person in the group and across from the quietest. Use eye contact to encourage quieter people to speak up. Serve and hear from everyone.
+ Listening in Bible study is just as important as talking. Evaluate each week. Did everyone share? Am I a good listener? Did I really hear what others shared? Was I attentive or distracted? Did I affirm others? Did I talk too much?
+ Share the overall goal aloud with all of the members of the group. Encourage each person in the group share aloud each time the group meets.
+ Make sure that people share answers only for those questions on which they have written answers. Don't just share off the top of your head. Really study.

Invite and Welcome Priests and Religious

Ask for the blessing of your pastor before you begin this study. Invite priests, deacons, and religious to come and pray with Bible study members, periodically answer questions from the question box, or give a wrap-up lecture. Accept whatever they can offer to the Bible study group. However, don't expect or demand anything from them. Appreciate that they are very busy and don't add additional burdens to their schedule. Accept with gratitude whatever is offered.

Wrap-Up Lecture

Additional information is available for this study in videotaped lectures filmed at EWTN studios, which can be obtained from Emmaus Road Publishing, 601 Granard Parkway, Steubenville, Ohio, 43952. You can obtain DVDs of these lectures by going to www.emmausroad.org or by calling 1-800-398-5470. Videotaped lectures may be used in addition to, or in place of, a wrap-up lecture, depending on your needs.

When offering a closing lecture, the presenter should spend extra time in prayer and study to prepare a good, sound lecture. Several people could take turns giving wrap-up lectures.

In Sacred Scripture are found elements, both implicit and explicit, which allow a vision of the human being and the world, which has exceptional philosophical density. Christians have come to an ever deeper awareness of the wealth to be found in the sacred text. It is there that we learn that what we experience is not absolute: it is neither uncreated nor self-generating. God alone is the Absolute. From the Bible there emerges also a vision of man as *imago Dei*. This vision offers indications regarding man's life, his freedom and the immortality of the human spirit. Since the created world is not self-sufficient, every illusion of autonomy which would deny the essential dependence on God of every creature—the human being included—leads to dramatic situations which subvert the rational search for the harmony and the meaning of human life.

Pope Saint John Paul II, *Fides et Ratio*, September 14, 1998, 80

A Prayer to the Holy Spirit

O Holy Spirit, Beloved of my soul, I adore You,
enlighten, guide, strengthen, and console me.
Tell me what I ought to say and do, and command me to do it.
I promise to be submissive in everything You will ask of me,
and to accept all that You permit to happen to me,
only show me what is Your will.
Amen.

CHAPTER 1

Annunciations
Luke 1

The Holy Spirit will come upon you,
and the power of the Most High will overshadow you;
therefore the child to be born will be called holy, the Son of God.
Luke 1:35

Luke addresses his Gospel to *Theophilus*, Greek for "lover of God," and explains his purpose for writing. *Inasmuch as many have undertaken to compile a narrative of the things which have been accomplished among us, just as they were delivered to us by those who from the beginning were eyewitnesses and ministers of the word, it seemed good to me also, having followed all things closely for some time past, to write an orderly account for you, most excellent Theophilus, that you may know the truth concerning the things of which you have been informed* (Luke 1:1–4). Whether Theophilus represents an actual person, or addresses any person who seeks after God in order to love Him more, one can prayerfully ponder.

Both Matthew—*now when Jesus was born in Bethlehem of Judea in the days of Herod the king* (Matthew 2:1) and Luke—*in the days of Herod, king of Judea* (Luke 1:5), identify a specific time in history for the births of John the Baptist and Jesus of Nazareth. Herod the Great of Judea ruled from 37–4 BC. After the birth of Jesus, this same Herod, in a furious rage, slaughtered all the male infants in Bethlehem, attempting to destroy the newborn King of the Jews (Matthew 2:1–18). Three decades later, in AD 29, the son of Herod actually does meet the King of the Jews. Herod questions and then treats Jesus with contempt and mockery, during His Passion preceding the crucifixion (Luke 23:8–11).

Angels are spiritual, immortal creatures with intelligence and free will, who glorify God and serve as envoys. Sometimes angels appear as humans. Often they appear in ways that inspire awe or fear in people. After the Fall, God drove Adam and Eve out of the Garden and *placed the cherubim, and a flaming sword which turned every way, to guard the way to the tree of life* (Genesis 3:24). In Tobit, Raphael appears disguised as the kinsman Azarias, accompanying Tobias on his travels, offering healing and deliverance, and later revealing his true identity. *I am Raphael, one of the seven holy angels who present the prayers of the saints and enter into the presence of the glory of the Lord* (Tobit 12:15). At the end of the Bible, God sends His messenger with a revelation to the Apostle John on the island of Patmos, and John falls at the angel's feet in fear, as though dead (Revelation 1:1–18).

Archangel Gabriel appears twice at the beginning of the New Testament: to the priest Zechariah in the temple and later to the Virgin Mary in Nazareth. The Gospel of Luke begins and ends in the temple. Zechariah is burning incense in the temple of the Lord when the angel appears (Luke 1:8–11). And after the Ascension of Jesus into heaven, the disciples *returned to Jerusalem with great joy, and were continually in the temple blessing God* (Luke 24:52–53). Luke's Gospel also begins and ends with joy. The angel announces to Zechariah, *and you will have joy and gladness, and many will rejoice at his birth* (Luke 1:14), and the disciples had joy at Jesus' Ascension (Luke 24:52).

Zechariah and Elizabeth—Elderly and childless, both come from the priestly tribe of Aaron. *And they were both righteous before God, walking in all the commandments and ordinances of the Lord blamelessly. But they had no child, because Elizabeth was barren, and both were advanced in years* (Luke 1:6–7). They demonstrate piety in their practice of Judaism. Righteousness indicates one who is holy in his heart, and adheres to the divine law. Later in Luke's Gospel, the centurion at the foot of the Cross will declare Jesus innocent or righteous (Luke 23:47). Luke also describes Joseph of Arimathea as *a good and righteous man* (Luke 23:50). While many people might be seen as righteous in another's eyes, Zechariah and Elizabeth are righteous in God's eyes! In Old Testament theology, God blesses good people with children. Childlessness was a sorrow shared by Sarah (Genesis 16), Rebekah (Genesis 25), Rachel (Genesis 29:31), and Hannah (1 Samuel 1–2). Modern readers note that while the cause of sterility could be either a husband or a wife, in this case, Elizabeth carries the blame for the infertility. And, they cannot understand why righteous people suffer!

Biblical names point to the action of God in the lives of His people.

Zechariah's name means "The Lord has remembered."
Elizabeth's name indicates "My God is fullness."
The Archangel Gabriel's name means "God is my warrior."
John's name means "God has shown favor."
Mary's name means "Excellence."
The Name above all names, **Jesus**, means **"God saves."**

Gabriel's Annunciations—The Archangel Gabriel brings two parallel annunciations in the first chapter of Luke. Each annunciation foretells:

1) the birth of a son;
2) the name chosen for the son; and
3) the destiny or vocation of the child.

In the Jerusalem temple, Gabriel announces to Zechariah: *Do not be afraid, Zechariah, for your prayer is heard, and your wife Elizabeth will bear you a son, and you shall call his name John. . . . And he will turn many of the sons of Israel to the Lord their God, and he will go before him in the spirit and power of Elijah, to turn the hearts of the fathers to the children, and the disobedient to the wisdom of the just, to make ready for the Lord a people prepared* (Luke 1:13, 16–17). Zechariah cannot believe this amazingly good news. He and Elizabeth are elderly. Zechariah needs proof. But God gives Zechariah the gift of silence in which to ponder the Almighty and reflect on the incomprehensible ways and mysteries of God.

Annunciation to the Virgin Mary (First Joyful Mystery)—In the little, obscure town of Nazareth, with a population of only about one hundred and fifty people, an extraordinary event unfolds that will impact the entire course of human history. Artists love to paint their impressions of the Annunciation of the Angel Gabriel to Mary. Fra Angelico painted many, and some show Mary at prayer with a book on her lap. Obviously, there were no books at this time in history, only scrolls. And only the wealthy or rabbis in the synagogue would own scrolls, not a poor single girl. Yet, the artist attempts to show Mary at prayer, perhaps praying for the coming of the Messiah to Israel. But the text does not reveal this. Gabriel could have appeared while Mary was sleeping, walking, working, or playing. She was just a very young girl.

Mary was *a virgin betrothed to a man whose name was Joseph, of the house of David* (Luke 1:27). Israel was awaiting a Davidic Messiah to fulfill the promise that God had made to King David: *I will establish the throne of his kingdom for ever. . . . And your house and your kingdom shall be made sure for ever before me; your throne shall be established for ever* (2 Samuel 7:13, 16). So when Gabriel announces that Jesus *will be great, and will be called the Son of the Most High; and the Lord God will give to him the throne of his father David . . . and of his kingdom there will be no end* (Luke 1:32–33), God's promise to David is fulfilled in Jesus.

Gabriel greets Mary in the words that most Catholics say every day: *Hail, full of grace, the Lord is with you!* (Luke 1:28). The early Church Fathers believed that this singular greeting showed that all the divine graces reposed in the Virgin Mary, and that she was free from original sin from the moment of her conception in the womb of her mother, Saint Anne. Many people confuse the Immaculate Conception of Mary with the Virgin Birth of Jesus. Mary was conceived through the loving embrace of a husband and wife, Saints Joachim and Anne. But, through a divine favor of God, she was preserved from original sin.

Dogma of the Immaculate Conception

The most Blessed Virgin Mary was, from the first moment of *her conception*, by a singular grace and privilege of almighty God and by virtue of the merits of Jesus Christ, Savior of the human race, preserved immune from all stain of original sin.
Pope Pius IX, Apostolic Constitution Defining the Immaculate Conception
Ineffabilis Deus (December 8, 1854)

Mary's virginity fulfills the prophecy of Isaiah: *Therefore the Lord himself will give you a sign. Behold, a virgin shall conceive and bear a son, and shall call his name Immanuel* (Isaiah 7:14). The Virgin birth shows God's absolute initiative in the Incarnation. The

Church proclaims "Mary's real and perpetual virginity even in the act of giving birth to the Son of God made man" (CCC 499). The Blessed Mother remains a virgin before, during, and after the birth of Jesus. Mary has only one biological child, Jesus, but her spiritual motherhood embraces all.

Unlike Zechariah, who doubted and demanded proof from the angel, Mary simply does not understand, but she still trusts God. Mary asks, *How can this be, since I have no husband?* (Luke 1:34). Actually, according to Jewish law, Mary does have a husband, because betrothal, a formal commitment ceremony, binds Joseph and Mary together before God. Matthew writes, *before they came together she was found to be with child of the Holy Spirit; and her husband Joseph, being a just man and unwilling to put her to shame, resolved to send her away quietly* (Matthew 1:18–19). Mary simply states and confirms her virginity. Even though, by Jewish law, Joseph is her husband, they have had no marital relations. The angel explains, *The Holy Spirit will come upon you, and the power of the Most High will overshadow you; therefore the child to be born will be called holy, the Son of God* (Luke 1:35). Both Matthew and Luke explain that Jesus is true God, by the power of the Holy Spirit, and true man, because He is the human Son of the Virgin Mary. This explanation suffices, and Mary gives her fiat: *Behold, I am the handmaid of the Lord; let it be to me according to your word* (Luke 1:38).

The Holy Spirit overshadows Mary—In the very beginning, *the Spirit of God was moving over the face of the waters* (Genesis 1:2) bringing things into being and giving them life. Now the Spirit of God overshadows Mary, bringing New Life to the world. The shadow or cloud indicates the divine presence in the midst of the people. When God gave Moses the Ten Commandments, a cloud covered Mount Sinai (Exodus 24:15–16). As the people wandered in the desert after the exodus from Egypt, a cloud led them along by day (Exodus 13:21ff), a cloud covered the ark of the covenant (Exodus 40:34–36), and God also appeared in a cloud upon the mercy seat (Leviticus 16:2). Mary exemplifies humility and obedience. She accepts the plan of God, even when she does not completely understand it. She trusts God and steps out in faith at the words of the angel.

The Visitation (Second Joyful Mystery)—Mary, a young, pregnant virgin goes in haste to visit her kinswoman Elizabeth in the hill country of Judah, now believed to be Ain Karim, a four-day walk. Do her parents or Joseph go with her? Elizabeth, filled with the Holy Spirit greets Mary: *Blessed are you among women, and blessed is the fruit of your womb!* (Luke 1:42). Elizabeth's greeting, so similar to that of the Angel Gabriel, shows that saints and angels alike honor Mary. She is more revered than Sarah, Ruth, Judith, Esther, or any of the holy women of old. The unborn John leaps for joy in his mother's womb (Luke 1:44). Recall David leaping and dancing before the Lord as the ark was brought to Jerusalem. *As the ark of the LORD came into the city of David, Michal the daughter of Saul looked out of the window, and saw King David leaping and dancing before the LORD* (2 Samuel 6:16). At this point, Mary prays one of the most beautiful prayers of the Church, the Magnificat, or Mary's Canticle, prayed and sung over the centuries in evening prayer all over the world. Similar to Hannah's Prayer, Mary praises and exalts the Lord. Mary's Canticle introduces the Lucan theme of prayer in this Gospel.

Hannah's Prayer

My heart exults in the LORD;
   my strength is exalted in the LORD.
My mouth derides my enemies, because
   I rejoice in your salvation.
There is none holy like the LORD,
   there is none besides you;
   there is no rock like our God.
Talk no more so very proudly, let not
   arrogance come from your mouth;
for the LORD is a God of knowledge,
   and by him actions are weighed.
The bows of the mighty are broken,
   but the feeble gird on strength.
Those who were full have hired
     themselves out for bread,
   but those who were hungry have
     ceased to hunger.
The barren has borne seven, but
   she who has many children is forlorn.
The LORD kills and brings to life; he
   brings down to Sheol and raises up.
The LORD makes poor and makes rich;
   he brings low, he also exalts.
He raises up the poor from the dust; he
   lifts the needy from the dung heap,
to make them sit with princes
   and inherit a seat of honor.
For the pillars of the earth are the LORD'S,
   and on them he has set the world.
He will guard the feet of his faithful
   ones; but the wicked shall be cut off
   in darkness; for not by might shall a
   man prevail.
The adversaries of the LORD shall be
   broken to pieces; against them he
   will thunder in heaven.
The LORD will judge the ends of the earth;
he will give strength to his king, and
   exalt the power of his anointed.

                    (1 Samuel 2:1–10)

Mary's Magnificat

My soul magnifies the Lord, and my
   spirit rejoices in God my Savior,
for he has regarded the low estate of
   his handmaiden.

For behold, henceforth all generations
   will call me blessed;
for he who is mighty has done great
   things for me,
   and holy is his name.

And his mercy is on those who fear
   him from generation to generation.

He has shown strength with his arm,
   he has scattered the proud in the
     imagination of their hearts,
   he has put down the mighty from
     their thrones,
   and exalted those of low degree;
he has filled the hungry with good
   things, and the rich he has sent
   empty away.

He has helped his servant Israel,
   in remembrance of his mercy,
as he spoke to our fathers,
   to Abraham and to his posterity
     for ever.

                    (Luke 1:46–55)

Look at the prayers of Hannah and Mary side by side, and consider the similarities and differences between each prayer. The humility and piety of Mary emerges in her Magnificat. Mary shows no vengeance toward any enemies. The maternal intercessor provides a prayer for all people through the ages. Then, Mary leaves Elizabeth before the birth of the baby John, and returns to her home.

John the Baptist is born—Surprisingly, on the eighth day after his birth, the day of circumcision, Elizabeth gives her son the name that the angel has spoken to her husband. How does she know his name? Has Zechariah communicated it to her in writing or in sign language? Has the Holy Spirit prompted her? When Zechariah confirms the name in writing, his tongue is loosed and he praises God in prophecy, in the prayer that the Church uses for morning prayer, the Canticle of Zechariah.

The Canticle of Zechariah

Blessed be the Lord, the God of Israel; he has come to his people and set them free.
  He has raised up for us a mighty savior, born of the house of his servant David.

Through his holy prophets he promised of old that he would save us from our
  enemies, from the hands of all who hate us.

He promised to show mercy to our fathers and to remember his holy covenant.

This was the oath he swore to our father Abraham; to set us free from the hands
  of our enemies, free to worship him without fear,
  holy and righteous in his sight all the days of our life.

You my child, shall be called the prophet of the Most High, for you will go before
  the Lord to prepare his way, to give his people knowledge of salvation
  by the forgiveness of their sins.

In the tender compassion of our God the dawn from on high shall break upon us,
  to shine on those who dwell in darkness and the shadow of death,
  and to guide our feet into the way of peace.

(Luke 1:68–79)

The Archangel Gabriel gives two annunciations, reported in Luke 1. In the temple in Jerusalem, the priest Zechariah receives the good news of the birth of his son, John the Baptist. By the end of Luke 1, this prophetic announcement is fulfilled, and Zechariah and Elizabeth are filled with joy. In the small town of Nazareth, Gabriel gives a more important Annunciation to the Virgin Mary. A miraculous conception will take place, as the Holy Spirit overshadows the Virgin Mary and prepares her to give birth to Jesus, true God and true Man, Immanuel, the Savior of the World.

1. Identify some functions of angels in the Bible.

Tobit 12:15ff
Luke 1:11ff, 26ff
Revelation 12:7ff
CCC 331–333

2. When, and by whom, was John the Baptist filled with the Holy Spirit?

Luke 1:15, 41
CCC 717

3. What can you learn about John the Baptist?

Luke 1:57–66
CCC 523
CCC 718–719
CCC 2684

4. What happened to Zechariah because of his doubts? Luke 1:20–23

5. Compare the following verses.

Isaiah 7:14
Luke 1:26–30

6. What does *full of grace* mean? Luke 1:28

CCC 490–491
CCC 492–493

7. What does the name *Jesus* mean? Luke 1:31

CCC 430
CCC 2812

8. Explain the significance of the Virgin birth. Luke 1:34–36

CCC 494, 496
CCC 499
CCC 504–506

9. What can you learn from Genesis 18:14 and Luke 1:37?

* Have you ever faced a seemingly impossible situation? What happened?

10. What does Mary's fiat signify?

Luke 1:38
CCC 148
CCC 273

11. Explain the drama in Luke 1:39–46.

12. Who leaped or danced before the Lord?

2 Samuel 6:16
Luke 1:44

13. Note some differences in Hannah's and Mary's canticles.

1 Samuel 2:1–10	Luke 1:46–55

14. What is your favorite verse in Mary's canticle? Luke 1:46–55

15. What had God promised? Genesis 17:7; Micah 7:20

16. Explain the drama in Luke 1:57–66.

17. When he can finally speak again, what does Zechariah do? Luke 1:67

18. What is your favorite verse in Zechariah's prophecy? Luke 1:68–79

19. What promise does Zechariah's prophecy reiterate? CCC 706

20. What did John the Baptist do then? Luke 1:80

* What impact does Mary's example of obedience have on your spiritual life?

CHAPTER 2

Birth of Jesus
Luke 2

And she gave birth to her first-born son
and wrapped him in swaddling cloths,
and laid him in a manger, because there was no place for them in the inn.
Luke 2:7

In those days a decree went out from Caesar Augustus that all the world should be enrolled (Luke 2:1). Luke's second chapter begins by citing Caesar Augustus, the founder of the Roman imperial system. At the time of this writing, the Julio-Claudian family has held the throne for over a hundred years, but even later, emperors would continue to use the titles of Caesar and Augustus. Luke shows that, in God's plan, the Romans too had a role to play in the coming of the Messiah.

Dating of the census presents a well-known chronological problem. In Luke 1:5, these events occur in the days of Herod, but now Luke connects the census with the governorship of Quirinius (Luke 2:2). However, Quirinius did not arrive until ten years after the death of Herod. Later, Luke shows good familiarity with the events of the Quirinial period (Acts 5:37, agreeing with Josephus, *Jewish Wars* vii.8,1 and *Antiquities of the Jews* xviii.1, xx.5,2). How can this seeming self-contradiction on Luke's part be resolved? The translation reads "first enrollment," which means that there must have been two or more. In Italian, however, the word *prima* means "before," and if such an idiom were at work here, the second verse would mean, "This enrollment took place first, before Quirinius became governor of Syria."

He was of the house and lineage of David (Luke 2:4). Jewish readers knew that only the House of David (Judeans) had the right to rule in the Holy Land, and that the House of Maccabee (Levites) and House of Herod (Idumeans) had been ruling for the past two centuries without a divine mandate. Roman readers had much less familiarity with this complex subject, but they knew that the Herodians held their throne only at the pleasure of the Julio-Claudian rulers in Rome. So, Luke walks a fine line here, stressing that Joseph and Jesus have the right to kingship without seeming to challenge the Roman authorities. Still, the Jews seize every chance to show the Romans that they had appointed the wrong king for Judea and Samaria. Politely, but clearly, Luke makes his theological point, that Jesus Christ is the true heir to the kingship of Israel, as part of the patrimony that He receives through Joseph's line. Luke's full roster of the lineage of David will be tabulated in the course of the next chapter (Luke 3:23–38).

The Nativity (Third Joyful Mystery)—*And Joseph also went up from Galilee, from the city of Nazareth, to Judea, to the city of David, which is called Bethlehem, because he was of the house and lineage of David, to be enrolled with Mary his betrothed, who was* *with child. And while they were there, the time came for her to be delivered. And she gave birth to her first-born son and wrapped him in swaddling cloths, and laid him in a manger, because there was no place for them in the inn* (Luke 2:4–7). The Messiah, the King of the Jews, chooses to be born in abject poverty and isolation. Beautiful Nativity cards and touching Christmas pageants can obscure the fact that Mary and Joseph were poor, alone, homeless, and unwelcomed in Bethlehem. The King of kings could have chosen to be born in a palace in luxury, but He decided on obscurity. He chooses to identify humbly with the poor, in a lonely and desolate place.

Bethlehem means "house of bread." A manger, mentioned three times by Luke (2:7, 12, 16), is a box where fodder is put to feed livestock. Jesus, *the bread of life* (John 6:35) begins His infant life in a feed trough, or breadbox. Later in Luke's Gospel, the disciples on the road to Emmaus will recognize Jesus in the breaking of the bread (24:30–32). Inns at this time were large public rooms where animals slept on one level and their owners slept above them, or in a room behind them. Synagogues also offered shelter to travelers. But, on this night, no one offers hospitality to Joseph and his pregnant wife Mary. Similarly, people today can refuse hospitality to others. There is no room for the inconvenient unborn child, the handicapped, or the elderly infirm. Some still refuse to welcome Jesus. Increasingly, society insists that there is no room for God in schools, courthouses, or in the public square.

Although no one shows Jesus hospitality at His birth, later in Luke's Gospel, Jesus will show hospitality to His Apostles in a guest room at an inn (22:11). And at His Last Supper, Jesus *took bread, and when he had given thanks he broke it and gave it to them, saying, "This is my body which is given for you. Do this in remembrance of me"* (22:19). Jesus continues to show hospitality to believers, giving His Body and Blood in the Eucharist for the nourishment of needy pilgrims.

Shepherds—*And in that region there were shepherds out in the field, keeping watch over their flock by night* (Luke 2:8). Jewish readers knew that David had tended sheep in those same fields, when he was anointed king, but the tribes still had to acclaim him before he could take the throne. So these shepherds have a role to play by accepting Jesus as their sovereign. Shepherds held the lowest social rank, like the *plebs* in Rome. Plebeians had no role in governance, but had won the veto power. The tribune, who represented the people, had only one word to say, *Veto!* "I forbid," to prevent any measure from becoming law. Modern veto powers derive from this ancient system, and are meant to ensure that laws are enacted with "the consent of the governed." So, here, the presence of the adoring shepherds before their newborn king has legal standing, signifying that those who will be ruled have accepted the authority of their ruler. To the Romans, this sort of comity was considered essential to the functioning of the state.

Similarly, in Church doctrine, the bishops are the ultimate teachers of dogma, but parents are the first teachers of the faith, followed by catechists, pastors, seminary professors, and theologians. Supernatural gifts of wisdom, understanding, counsel, fortitude, knowledge, piety, and fear of the Lord inhere in the whole Church by the gift of the

Holy Spirit. A consensus of faith and morals unites the Church with the supreme head, Christ Himself. Papal teaching requires a response, which happens when the faithful grant interior assent of the will, called *sensus fidelium*, "the sense of the faithful." This pious concord of truth already existed in the hearts of the shepherds of Bethlehem, and has continued to grow ever since through the ministrations of divine grace. The proof of heavenly wisdom is very simple, the instinct to worship the Christ Child.

Angels—*And the angel said to them, "Be not afraid; for behold, I bring you good news of a great joy which will come to all the people"* (Luke 2:10). The words *I bring you good news* are in Greek *evangelizomay humin*, literally: "I evangelize you." The word *gospel* comes from this verb. The first evangelists in the Gospel of Luke are the angels, who proclaim a "Gospel of great joy." There is no such thing as a gospel of bad news; the whole Gospel is good news. Even Gospel warnings exist to help the listeners avoid actions that would cause suffering to themselves or others. Theological joy is also recognized in Canon Law, which says that the faithful are to abstain on Sundays and holy days from any works or affairs that hinder "the joy proper to the Lord's day" (1983 Code, canon 1247).

Glory to God in the highest, and on earth peace among men with whom he is pleased (Luke 2:14). This angelic canticle contains two elements, the first invoking divine glory and the second invoking earthly peace. Luke's Jewish readers knew the Hebrew greeting *shalom*, "peace," and that these angels were saluting the whole earth, as the archangel Gabriel had saluted the Virgin Mary. Everyone understood that, although the imperial armed forces had imposed *pax romana*, the "Roman peace," the angels had announced *pax hominibus*, a "peace for all humanity."

The early Church loved this angelic canticle so much that it expanded this prayer, as it did with the Hail Mary. In its longer form, the Gloria would become the first liturgical hymn of the Church. Shortly after AD 100, Governor Pliny the Younger wrote to Emperor Trajan to ask advice about what to do with all the Christians, who were already a large proportion of the population in the province of Asia. Pliny described how, at regular intervals (once a week), Christians would sing a morning hymn in honor of their God. Liturgical scholars assume that the reference is to the Gloria, which originally formed part of Matins, but eventually was attached to Mass except during the penitential seasons of Advent and Lent.

The repertory of Gregorian Chant contains a number of different musical settings for the Latin text of the Gloria, also called *Laus angelorum*, or "The Angels' Praise." The Gloria of Mass XVI transcribes an ancient Byzantine melody, originally sung to the original Greek text (*Kyriale*, Solesmes edition 1997, p. 55).

The Presentation (Fourth Joyful Mystery)—*[They] offer a sacrifice according to what is said in the law of the Lord, "a pair of turtledoves, or two young pigeons"* (Luke 2:24, quoting Leviticus 12:8). Luke is the only source for the Fourth Joyful Mystery, the Presentation of the Child Jesus in the Temple, celebrated each year on February 2.

This passage shows the poverty of the Holy Family. Jewish readers, many of whom were parents themselves, knew the fuller quotation from Leviticus, *and if she cannot afford a lamb, then she shall take two turtledoves or two young pigeons* (12:8). The wealthy were to bring a lamb and one bird, but the poor were allowed to bring two birds instead. Two lines of new parents formed at the temple, the wealthy in fine clothes carrying a newborn and a bird, and leading a lamb, while through another entrance the poor were carrying a newborn and two birds. Joseph, Mary, and Jesus were in the procession of the poor. Those looking for the coming Messiah would have done well to concentrate their attention on the line-up of the poor, as indeed were the prophetic Simeon and Anna.

The Glory of Israel—*For my eyes have seen your salvation* (Luke 2:30). Simeon, whose name means "God has heard," and Anna, whose name means "Grace," represent the *anawim*, the humble people who yearn for the coming of the Messiah and rejoice to see His day. The poor people teach Luke's Roman readers that Jesus is *a light of revelation to the Gentiles* (2:32), and they teach Luke's Jewish readers that Jesus is the *glory to your people Israel* (2:32). They provide the continuity of faith, hope, and love between the Old and New Testaments.

Simeon continues the Lucan prayer theme by providing a beautiful prayer, the Nunc Dimittis, which is the Gospel Canticle to close evening prayer in the Liturgy of the Hours. Thus, Luke recounts another prayer that the Church has chosen to include in the Divine Office to be sung, chanted, or prayed around the world nightly. Compare the prayer below from the Liturgy of the Hours with Luke 2:29–32.

Nunc Dimittis

Lord, now you let your servant go in peace;
your word has been fulfilled:
my own eyes have seen the salvation
which you have prepared in the sight of every people:
a light to reveal you to the nations
and the glory of your people Israel.

The pairings of Simeon and Anna, along with Zechariah and Elizabeth, show that man and woman stand together, side-by-side, before God, with equal dignity. Saint John Paul II highlighted this truth in his teaching on the *Theology of the Body*. Men and women are equal in honor and grace, enjoy similar gifts and talents, and have the same opportunity to respond to God's grace and invitation, or to reject it. Men and women have equal responsibility to be docile to the Holy Spirit and use the graces and charisms given by God to advance His kingdom on the face of the earth. Luke highlights this truth throughout his Gospel in his treatment of women.

The Finding in the Temple (Fifth Joyful Mystery)—*Now his parents went to Jerusalem every year at the feast of the Passover* (Luke 2:41). Luke is the only source for the Fifth Joyful Mystery, the Finding of the Child Jesus in the Temple. The Torah obliges Jewish men to assemble for public sacrifice on three high holy days: Passover, Pentecost, and Tabernacles. Before Solomon built the temple in Jerusalem, sacrifices were offered wherever the ark was then located. When the northern tribes broke away, northerners and southerners gathered separately. After the exile, Jews gathered in Jerusalem and Samaritans gathered on Mount Gerizim.

Inhabitants of Jerusalem were able to attend all three assemblies every year. Those from far away lands, like Spain, might consider themselves fortunate to attend once in their lives. The Galilean and Syrian Jews had to pass through hostile Samaritan territory, and cross paths with the Samaritan pilgrims assembling at Gerizim. Historian Josephus records many cases of conflict and violence at pilgrimage time. Pilgrims traveled in convoys for mutual protection. Luke relates that the Holy Family attended the Passover feast in Jerusalem every year.

Mary and Joseph probably waited until Jesus was about six years of age before they began to go annually to Jerusalem, because the dangers were too great for a small child. From that time onward, the holy day was a happily anticipated annual family reunion for extended families. Perhaps, the child John traveled along with his parents, Zechariah and Elizabeth, who were part of the temple priestly group. Each year, perhaps the young Jesus visited with John, and Mary may have visited with her elder cousin Elizabeth again. It may have been like the Visitation on an annual basis.

Around the year AD 8 or so, Jesus and John both reached their twelfth birthdays and made bar mitzvah. They were now considered men. As boys, their attendance had been optional, but now they attend the festival with pride in fulfillment of their mature obligations. John and Jesus could read from the scroll of the prophets, displaying their skills in the Hebrew language. Jesus must have displayed particular brilliance in reading in the temple, as He did in the synagogue in Nazareth (Luke 4:16). The teachers in the temple asked Jesus to read and explain more. They could not seem to reach the end of His wisdom, which mystified them because they did not know who His teacher had been. His Teacher had hung the stars in the sky!

This joyful mystery started out as a sorrowful mystery, because Mary and Joseph could not find Jesus among their group on their way home. Mary asks: *why have you treated us so?* (Luke 2:48), a question that many others throughout the ages have asked God. Jesus had to be about His father's business, but was that the business of Joseph? Or was it the business of God the Father, a term Jesus uses fifteen times in Luke's Gospel (Luke 2:49; 6:36; 9:26; 10:21a; 10:21b; 10:22; 11:2; 11:13; 12:30; 12:32; 22:29; 22:42; 23:34; 23:46; 24:49)? Such vocabulary rarely appears in the Hebrew Bible. This language does not exist in other world religions. Christians are accustomed to calling God "Father," but before Jesus taught in the temple, such talk about God as Father was rare. Jesus elevated it to high profile and taught His disciples to pray, *"Our Father who art in heaven"* (Matthew 6:9) and *"Father, hallowed be your name"* (Luke 11:2). Mary and Joseph did not understand Jesus' response to them. Faith requires trust. Even when life remains a mystery and you cannot understand God, trust Him.

And Jesus increased in wisdom and in stature, and in favor with God and man (Luke 2:52). The body and mind of Jesus experienced growth just like everyone else's, because His humanity was real. As the Divine Praises pray, "Blessed be Jesus Christ, true God and true man." It is not easy for us to *have the mind of Christ* (1 Corinthians 2:16), because sometimes He speaks like God, and sometimes He speaks like man. So we often reach too high and miss the man, or reach too low and miss the God. Note, however, that the human mind of Christ, unencumbered by sin and in lasting union with the Divine Mind, was capable of greater thoughts than any other human mind. Jesus was a true genius, and His was no commonplace mind. His human mind held the supernatural gift of wisdom in its purest form.

---

1. Why was Jesus born in Bethlehem? Micah 5:2

2. What does a first-born son signify?

Exodus 13:1
Luke 2:7
CCC 500
CCC 501

3. Explain the Christmas mystery. Luke 2:7; CCC 525

* What is your favorite Christmas memory?

4. Explain the drama in Luke 2:8–14.

* What Christmas carols best explain the Christmas mystery to you?

5. Compare the following verses.

Luke 2:14	
Luke 19:38	

6. What did the shepherds do after hearing the angel? Luke 2:15–19

7. What is the significance of the angel's announcement? CCC 437

8. Explain and number how Jesus is progressively made manifest. CCC 486

9. What does Mary do? Why is this useful? Luke 2:19; CCC 2599

10. What do the shepherds do? Luke 2:20

11. What is the significance of the circumcision of Jesus?

Luke 2:21
CCC 527

12. Explain the significance of the Presentation in the Temple.

Luke 2:22–32
CCC 529
CCC 583

13. Who did Joseph and Mary meet in the temple? Luke 2:25, 36

14. What can you learn from the following verses?

Isaiah 42:6b; 49:6b
Isaiah 52:10b
Luke 2:29–32

15. What did Simeon say to Mary? Luke 2:34–35

16. What would this mean? John 19:25–27; CCC 149

17. Where did Jesus grow up? Luke 2:39–40

18. What does the hidden life of Jesus invite? CCC 531–533

19. Explain the drama in Luke 2:41–51. CCC 534

20. What virtue does Jesus possess? Luke 2:52; Sirach 1:1, 5, 9

* Who is your wisest friend? How can you get wisdom? Sirach 1:20, 26–27

Monthly Social Activity

This month, your small group will meet for coffee, tea, or a simple breakfast, lunch, or dessert in someone's home. Pray for this social event and for the host or hostess. Try, if at all possible, to attend.

Read again the Nativity story in Luke 2. Share about one of the following aspects of Christmas.

Some examples:

◆ *I was in a Christmas pageant once...*

◆ *My favorite Christmas memory is...*

◆ *One Christmas tradition that I enjoy is...*

CHAPTER 3

Prepare the Way
Luke 3

"The voice of one crying in the wilderness:
Prepare the way of the Lord, make his paths straight."
Luke 3:4, quoting Isaiah 40:3

John the Baptist calls for conversion—Luke arrives here at the point where the Gospel of Mark begins, at the public ministry of John the Baptist. All three synoptic Gospels contain this same quotation, but Luke incorporates a longer portion of the source material, adding the verses: *Every valley shall be filled, and every mountain and hill shall be brought low, and the crooked shall be made straight, and the rough ways shall be made smooth; and all flesh shall see the salvation of God* (Luke 3:5–6, quoting Isaiah 40:4–5). Why is Luke so taken by this prophecy?

First, *the way of the Lord* in Lucan terminology is a synonym for the Christian movement itself, and it will appear again exactly as such later (Acts 18:25). The witness of John counterbalances the negative testimony of the high priestly class.

Second, because the longer quotation contains a universal aspect: *And the glory of the LORD shall be revealed, and all flesh shall see it together* (Isaiah 40:5). Luke condenses this verse to read *"and all flesh shall see the salvation of God"* (Luke 3:6). For Luke's Jewish readers, the longer quotation reminds them that the Jews were called to form a light to the nations. For Gentile readers, the longer quote invites them to see the salvation wrought in Christ Jesus for all sinners. The influence of Pauline theology is clear in the Lucan approach to the material, that John the Baptist set forth a path upon which Jesus would tread to illumine all the nations.

> John is the voice, the Lord is *the Word who was in the beginning.* John is the voice that lasts for a time; from the beginning Christ is the Word who lives for ever. . . . *The voice of one crying in the wilderness* is the voice of one breaking the silence. *Prepare the way for the Lord,* he says, as though he were saying: "I speak out in order to lead Him into your hearts, but He does not choose to come where I lead Him unless you prepare the way for Him." *To prepare the way* means to pray well; it means thinking humbly of oneself. . . . He *[John]* understood that he was a lamp, and his fear was that it might be blown out by the wind of pride.
> Saint Augustine of Hippo (354–430), *Sermon,* 13. 293, 3

Prepare the way—*And he answered them, "He who has two coats, let him share with him who has none; and he who has food, let him do likewise"* (Luke 3:11). Only Luke recounts the specific instructions that John gave, first to the multitudes, next to the tax collectors, and then to the soldiers (3:10–14). What was Luke's source for this additional material? Among those who heard John the Baptist preach were pilgrims from around the world, including Apollos from Alexandria (Acts 18:24–27) and twelve pilgrims from Ephesus (Acts 19:1–7). Luke had already joined Paul's group (Acts 16:14, when he begins to narrate in first-person plural), and would have had an extended opportunity to interview those twelve during the time that Paul spent in Ephesus, three months preaching in the synagogue (Acts 19:8) and two years outside the synagogue (Acts 19:10).

Tax collectors also came to be baptized, and said to him, "Teacher, what shall we do?" And he said to them, "Collect no more than is appointed you" (Luke 3:12–13). Gentiles would have been pleased to see that civil servants were not excluded from the way of the Lord. Jewish readers may have been more challenged. Tax collectors, called publicans, collaborated with the Roman occupying powers, handled the foreign currency with graven images of false gods, and often enriched themselves by overcharging. As a result, they found themselves excommunicated from the temple and synagogue. A hunger for holiness led many of them to be baptized by John, and later to follow Jesus. Luke mentions tax collectors more often than any other evangelist, and mentions two by name:
  — Levi, also known as Matthew from Capernaum (Luke 5:27, Matthew 9:9);
  — Zacchaeus from Jericho (Luke 19:2).

Soldiers also asked him, "And we, what shall we do?" And he said to them, "Rob no one by violence or by false accusation, and be content with your wages" (Luke 3:14). At the time Luke wrote, Roman soldiers were less popular than ever in the Holy Land, as events cascaded into the Judean War, leading to the destruction of Jerusalem. Jewish and Gentile readers alike discover that soldiers, too, could find a place on the *way of peace* (Luke 1:79). The ranks of enlisted men provided one of the seedbeds for the spread of Christianity in the Roman Empire. In the Acts of the Apostles, Luke gives the names of several of the first soldiers of high honor who assisted the Apostles and responded to the Gospel:
  — Cornelius, *a devout man who feared God with all his household* (Acts 10:2);
  — Claudius Lysias, who rescued Paul from the mob (Acts 23:26);
  — Julius, who escorted Paul and Luke on the prison ships (Acts 27:1).

The Baptism of Jesus—*Now when all the people were baptized, and when Jesus also had been baptized and was praying, the heaven was opened, and the Holy Spirit descended upon him in bodily form, as a dove, and a voice came from heaven, "You are my beloved Son; with you I am well pleased"* (Luke 3:21–22). Luke shows that the Holy Spirit baptizes Jesus, the same power who embodied Jesus since His conception (Luke 1:32, 35). This same Holy Spirit will embolden the disciples on Pentecost (Acts 2:1ff). The voice from heaven reveals God the Father.

Luke highlights the Blessed Trinity in his Gospel. God the Father speaks again at the Transfiguration (Luke 9:28–36) and is referenced fifteen times. Jesus thanks the Father (10:21), and teaches His disciples when they pray to begin by addressing God as Father:

"Father, hallowed be your name" (11:2). Jesus promises that the Father will give the Holy Spirit to those who ask him (11:13). At the end of His Passion, while Jesus is dying on the Cross for the sins of the whole world, He says *"Father, into your hands, I commit my spirit!" (23:46).*

The Angelic Doctor, Saint Thomas Aquinas explains the theological importance of the Baptism of the Lord, and its relationship to our own Christian Baptism.

When the time came for Him *[Jesus]* to teach, to work miracles and to draw men to Himself, then was it fitting for the Godhead to be attested to from on high by the Father's testimony, so that His teaching might be more credible: *"The Father who sent me has himself borne witness to me"* (John 5:37). . . . . Christ's baptism was the exemplar of our own. In it the mystery of the Blessed Trinity was revealed, and the faithful, on receiving Baptism, are consecrated by the invocation of and by the power of the Blessed Trinity. Similarly, heaven opening signifies that the power, the effectiveness of this sacrament, comes from above, from God, and that the baptized have the road to heaven opened up to them, a road which original sin had closed.

Saint Thomas Aquinas (1224–1274), *Summa Theologiae 3, 39, 3–8*

Theophany—The Baptism of Jesus manifests Our Lord's divinity and reveals the mystery of the Blessed Trinity. The Holy Spirit descends from heaven in the appearance of a dove, and God the Father speaks in a voice from above. This event constitutes a *Theophany*—a visible manifestation of God to all who have the eyes of faith and are willing to see and believe. The voice from heaven reiterates Old Testament promises: *"You are my son, today I have begotten you"* (Psalm 2:7), and *Behold my servant, whom I uphold, my chosen, in whom my soul delights; I have put my Spirit upon him, he will bring forth justice to the nations* (Isaiah 42:1).

Saint John Paul II encouraged believers to meditate on the Baptism of the Lord in praying the first Luminous Mystery of the Rosary. Sandwiched in these rich verses, one might miss the fact that Jesus was praying. *Jesus also had been baptized and was praying* (Luke 3:21). The public ministry of Jesus begins and ends with prayer. On the Mount of Olives, Jesus withdrew from His disciples, *and knelt down and prayed* (22:41). And from the Cross Jesus prayed to God for forgiveness for sinners: *Father, forgive them; for they know not what they do* (23:34).

Luke shows Jesus praying throughout His ministry. Prior to healing a paralytic, *He withdrew to the wilderness and prayed* (5:16). Before calling His Apostles, *He went out to the hills to pray, and all night he continued in prayer to God* (6:12). Jesus went up the mountain to pray before His Transfiguration (9:28). Our Lord was praying when the disciples asked for teaching on prayer (11:1ff). Jesus prays specifically for Peter, *I have prayed for you that your faith may not fail* (22:32). Jesus provides the impetus for Paul's exhortation to *pray constantly* (1 Thessalonians 5:17).

Jesus, when he began his ministry, was about thirty years of age, being the son (as was supposed) of Joseph (Luke 3:23). Luke's Roman readers would have seen the career of Jesus standing in parallel to that of their men of highest rank, who on their thirtieth birthdays donned patrician purple for the first time and took their seats in the senate chambers, to share in debates and cast their votes. Luke's Jewish readers knew that rabbis also began public ministry at the age of thirty, and would have assumed that the same was true of Jesus and of John the Baptist. Lucan chronology suggests that, as John the Baptist was six months older than Jesus, John would have started his ministry in June and Jesus in December.

The Ancestry of Jesus—*The son of Mattatha, the son of Nathan, the son of David* (Luke 3:31). Both Luke and Matthew provide paternal genealogies for Saint Joseph. Matthew traces the royal line through Solomon (Matthew 1:6), while Luke traces a collateral line through Nathan, both sons of David (Luke 3:31). Neither the Historiographer nor the Chronicler give us any biographical information about Nathan, but he is listed third and Solomon fourth of the sons of Bathsheba in the three surviving lists (2 Samuel 5:14; 1 Chronicles 3:5; 14:4). David passed over Nathan for the kingship in favor of his younger brother Solomon, but Nathan must have survived into adulthood and had a son, whose personal qualities were probably superior to those of his cousin Rehoboam, under whom the kingdom divided. Within the House of David there must have been a minority party loyal to the Nathanite line, and Luke passes on to us their royal list, which bypasses the checkered history of the Solomonic line. Luke provides the only surviving record of that collateral line, which rejoins the official line in the person of Saint Joseph.

The son of Adam, the son of God (Luke 3:38). Matthew's genealogy goes forwards from Abraham to David to Jechoniah to Joseph; Luke's genealogy goes backwards from Joseph, bypassing Jechoniah, but continuing back to David, to Abraham, to Adam, all the way back to God. Luke puts a Christological title, "son of God," at the end of the genealogy, naming God as the spiritual Father of the entire human race. Adam, a rightful son of God, forfeited his sonship through sin, while Jesus, at the head of the list, redeems the whole heritage. Jewish readers would identify with the powerful statement of Jesus' identity here, as heir to the divine kingship, and not just a human throne. Romans saw their leaders make efforts to trace their lineage back to the gods. The Lucan list affirms not just the human but also the divine identity of Jesus. Coming at the end of the long list of human parents, the divine parentage at the very end makes an extremely powerful theological statement.

Saint Paul comments on the significance of the new Adam. *Yet death reigned from Adam to Moses, even over those whose sins were not like the transgression of Adam, who was a type of the one who was to come. . . . If because of one man's trespass, death reigned through that one man, much more will those who receive the abundance of grace and the free gift of righteousness reign in life through the one man Jesus Christ* (Romans 5:14, 16). Jesus atones for the sin of Adam and for our sins.

Luke, who throughout his Gospel is keenly attentive to Jesus' prayer, and portrays him again and again at prayer—in conversation with the Father—tells us that Jesus was praying while he received Baptism (Luke 3:21). Looking at the events in light of the Cross and Resurrection, the Christian people realized what happened: Jesus loaded the burden of all mankind's guilt upon his shoulders; he bore it down into the depths of the Jordan. He inaugurated his public activity by stepping into the place of sinners. His inaugural gesture is an anticipation of the Cross. He is, as it were, the true Jonah who said to the crew of the ship, "Take me and throw me into the sea" (Jonah 1:12). The whole significance of Jesus' Baptism, the fact that he bears "all righteousness," first comes to light on the Cross: The Baptism is an acceptance of death for the sins of humanity, and the voice that calls out "This is my beloved Son" over the baptismal waters is an anticipatory reference to the Resurrection. This also explains why, in his own discourses, Jesus uses the word *baptism* to refer to his death (Mark 10:38; Luke 12:50).

Pope Benedict XVI, *Jesus of Nazareth* (New York: Doubleday, 2007), 18

1. What can you learn about John the Baptist?

Matthew 3:1–7
Mark 1:1–8
Luke 1:13–18
John 1:19–30

2. What does Jesus say about John the Baptist?

Matthew 11:7–10
Matthew 11:11–19

3. Where did John hear the word of God, and where did he go? Luke 3:2–3

4. Explain the prophecy of Isaiah.

Isaiah 40:3–5
Luke 3:4–6

5. Define "repentance." CCC 1490 What are *fruits that befit repentance*? Luke 3:8

6. How can a person make effective repentance today? CCC 1460

7. Compare the following verses.

Luke 3:9
Hebrews 6:7–8

* What evidence of good fruit would you hope to find in your life?

8. How does John advise the following groups of people? Luke 3:10–14

Multitudes	
Tax collectors	
Soldiers	

* Which one of the above suggestions could you enact in your life?

9. How does John the Baptist respond to people's expectations?

Luke 3:15–16	
Luke 3:17–18	

10. Why did John the Baptist get into trouble with Herod? Luke 3:19

Luke 3:19	
Mark 6:14–18	

11. How did Herodias get vengeance on John the Baptist? Mark 6:17–29

12. Explain the drama in Luke 3:21–22.

13. Identify the three persons of the Blessed Trinity in Luke 3:21–22.

14. What does Saint Luke emphasize in his Gospel? CCC 2600

15. What is manifested in the baptism of Jesus? CCC 535

16. Explain the role of submission in Jesus' life. CCC 536

17. How does one become assimilated to Jesus? CCC 537

18. How old was Jesus when He began His public life? Luke 3:23

19. Who in the genealogy of Jesus provides kingship? Luke 3:31; 2 Samuel 7:4–16

20. Who is the foster-father of Jesus and who is the real Father? Luke 3:23, 38

* Describe your earthly father, and choose one adjective for your heavenly Father.

CHAPTER 4

Temptations
Luke 4

And Jesus answered him, "It is written,
'Man shall not live by bread alone.'"
Luke 4:4

Temptation—After Jesus' baptism, with the Holy Spirit hovering like a dove over Him, He goes out into the desert and encounters the *unholy* spirit hovering over the dry land. The testing-place of Jesus in southern Judea falls on the edge of the same desert where Moses was tempted, at the place called Meribah or Massa. In fact, the word for temptation in Hebrew is *massa*, from the tempting-place of Moses. Hence, the temptations of Jesus would be called in Hebrew "the Massa of the Messiah," just as the teachings of Jesus have been called "the Torah of the Messiah." Among other parallels: As Moses spent forty years in the desert, Jesus spends forty days; as Moses tempted God while bringing water from the rock, Jesus was tempted to make bread from the rock; and all three of the answers that Jesus gives to the devil come from Deuteronomy, the fifth book in the Torah of Moses.

Jesus prepares to face *diabolos*, Greek for "the devil," with (1) prayer, (2) fasting, and (3) Sacred Scripture. Jesus overcomes the world, the flesh, and the devil. All people on earth are tested to prove their mettle against the forces of evil, to show whether they are part of the solution or part of the problem. Adam and Eve met the unholy spirit, and they failed us all. The Virgin Mary crushed the head of the ancient serpent under her heel. Jesus, too, had to be tested, so that His sacred humanity would be known to be real. *For we have not a high priest who is unable to sympathize with our weaknesses, but one who in every respect has been tempted as we are, yet without sinning* (Hebrews 4:15). Prayer, fasting, and Scripture memory can help His followers to resist temptations as well.

Devil Tempts Jesus	Jesus Prevails
➤ Make stones into bread (Luke 4:3)	➤ *"Man shall not live by bread alone"* (Luke 4:4; Deuteronomy 8:3)
➤ Worship me *[the devil]* (Luke 4:7)	➤ *"You shall worship the Lord your God, and him only shall you serve"* (Luke 4:8; Deuteronomy 6:13)
➤ Throw yourself down from the pinnacle of the temple (Luke 4:9)	➤ *"You shall not tempt the Lord your God"* (Luke 4:12; Deuteronomy 6:16)

Fasting from bread is part of the spirituality of many world religions. The fast days in Judaism lead up to the Day of Atonement at the end of September. Jesus very likely spent his forty days in the desert at the same time that other Jews were fasting as well, in August, when the desert was hottest. Later, when Jesus and His disciples were accused of not fasting, He said that they cannot fast while the bridegroom is present, but when the bridegroom is gone, then they will fast. On another occasion, He said that one should fast in private and not on public display for human praise.

Fasting and dieting are totally different. Dieting is for physical health, but fasting is for spiritual health. We may wish to feel a little of what the hungry people of the world feel, and hence to grow in empathy. We may join our fasting with that of Jesus in the desert, to have a share in His sufferings. Acts of penance, done in the right spirit, purify the soul and prepare us to celebrate the great mysteries.

Catholic rules of fasting and abstinence from meat have been greatly reduced. Formerly, Catholics fasted from midnight to prepare for Holy Communion; now they must fast for only one hour. Formerly, there were ninety days of abstinence and forty days of fasting in the year. Now there are only eight days of abstinence (Ash Wednesday and the seven Fridays of Lent, for those fourteen to fifty-nine years of age) and only two days of fasting (Ash Wednesday and Good Friday, for those twenty to fifty-nine).

Jesus answered him, "It is written, 'You shall worship the Lord your God, and him only shall you serve'" (Luke 4:8 quoting Deuteronomy 6:13). Mark covers the temptations in just two verses. Matthew has eleven verses and Luke twelve, and they both describe three temptations. Matthew ends with the First Commandment, *You shall worship the Lord your God* (Matthew 4:10), but Luke has it in the middle. This commandment is what the temptations are all about. All sin is rebellion against the One deserving worship—all sin amounts to idolatry. The devil wants our worship because he desires our destruction; God wants our worship because He desires our salvation. Thus all the laws are summarized in the great one, *You shall love the LORD your God with all your heart* (Deuteronomy 6:5), which a scribe will later quote to the approval of Jesus (Luke 10:27).

And Jesus answered him, "It is said, 'You shall not tempt the Lord your God'" (Luke 4:12, quoting Deuteronomy 6:16). The devil did not know with whom he was dealing in the desert. He does not call Jesus the Son of God, but twice says to Jesus, *If you are the Son of God* (Luke 4:3, 9). Remember that the devil promised Eve and Adam, *"you will be like God"* (Genesis 3:5). The devil thought Jesus was a fake and was trying to bring Him down. Jesus knew how real He was, and would later prove His powers in the gift of Himself in the Eucharist, but He resists any temptation to prove this to the devil. No one has to prove anything to the powers of evil.

Temptation is spiritual torture. To know what God wants but be pulled another way is like the rack. Most Christians fail to take the temptations of Jesus seriously, since they believe Him incapable of sin. Saint Teresa of Ávila wrote that the worst sufferings of

Jesus were spiritual (*Interior Castle* 5:2; *Way of Perfection* 42). The Pure and Holy One surrounded by sin and impurity for thirty-three years resulted in spiritual and emotional pain and suffering. Jesus had the power to strike down the devil in the desert, but the Father willed that He wait three more years to do so. Saint Teresa writes that physical suffering was a joy to Jesus, because it brought to an end the long period of waiting.

The Synagogue in Nazareth—*"The Spirit of the Lord is upon me, because he has anointed me to preach good news to the poor"* (Luke 4:18 quoting Isaiah 61:1). Jesus goes to the synagogue of Nazareth, His hometown. Luke provides a much longer pericope of fourteen verses, more than twice as long as the parallel accounts in Matthew and Mark. Luke's source for the extra material could be Mary herself, who would have attended the event, up in the women's gallery behind the veil. Other relatives of Jesus, perhaps some aunts, uncles, and cousins who went about with Mary, could also have been present. It should have been a happy day, like when the mother of a newly ordained priest or deacon hears him preach for the first time.

Jesus stands to read from the scroll of the prophet Isaiah, and then gives a comment. This reflects the order of the service in a synagogue, which begins with the Torah reading, followed by a reading from the prophets, and then a sermon. The Torah reader, one by one, pronounced each of the verses in Hebrew, and then gave an impromptu rendering into the vernacular. The prophetic reader read three verses at a time, first in the Hebrew and then in a spontaneous translation. Most likely Jesus followed this custom, first reading Isaiah in Hebrew, then translating it into Aramaic, and only then giving His homily.

The sermon excerpt is longer in Luke (seven verses) than in Mark or Matthew (one verse each). Jesus does more than explain the passage; He announces its fulfillment: *Today this scripture has been fulfilled in your hearing* (Luke 4:21). Isaiah prophesied what would happen when the Messiah came, and these are the very miracles that Jesus performs. At first everyone speaks well of Jesus, but then small-mindedness prevails. Jesus is the son of Joseph, the well-known carpenter, who had built their tables and doorposts. Where did the son of Joseph get all this wisdom?

Doubtless you will quote to me this proverb, "Physician, heal yourself" (Luke 4:23). Jesus can read hearts, but the facial expressions and the gestures are enough to tell Him that His audience is not with Him. Never one to back off from a confrontation, Jesus addresses their state of mind. All three of the synoptic evangelists quote the line, *No prophet is acceptable in his own country* (Luke 4:24; cf. Matthew 13:57; Mark 6:4), but only Luke has the previous line, *Physician, heal yourself*. Since Luke himself was a physician, this verse held more meaning for him than for the other evangelists. Physicians are mentioned more often in Luke, as taxes are mentioned more often in Matthew. One Egyptian manuscript (Oxyrhynchus Papyrus I.11) has an alternative version, *No physician performs cures on those who know him*. Neither version of this proverb can be found in the Hebrew Bible, and no other source has been found.

Only Luke relates that the crowd tried to throw Jesus off the cliff at the edge of Nazareth (Luke 4:29). Again, Mary as a source would have remembered any hostile pushing and jostling out in the street afterwards. From there Jesus proceeds to Capernaum, where the synagogue crowd gives Him a much better reception. There, Jesus worked His first two Lucan miracles on a Sabbath day, when He stilled and expelled a demon from a man in the synagogue (4:35), and then went to the home of Simon Peter and cured Peter's mother-in-law of a fever (4:39).

Jesus heals and drives out demons—After Jesus resisted the temptations of the devil in the wilderness, at the beginning of Luke 4, He now goes on the offensive and delivers people from demonic influence. Luke recounts Jesus performing four exorcisms (Luke 4:31–37; 8:26–39; 9:37–43; 13:10–17). Jesus vanquishes the power of evil through the power of the Holy Spirit and obedient faith.

In the synagogue there was a man with an unclean spirit. What was a man possessed by a demon doing in the synagogue? It still can surprise people to see the weeds growing among the wheat. No one expects to see evil encroaching upon the holy, or see sin in the church. The demon recognizes who Jesus is: *"I know who you are, the Holy One of God." But Jesus rebuked him, saying, "Be silent, and come out of him"* (Luke 4:34–35). Knowing who Jesus is intellectually is not enough. The demons had head knowledge about Jesus; however, faith requires repentance, trusting in Jesus, and coming to *know* Him, not just knowing *about* Him.

The demons attacked Jesus in the synagogue, and the worshippers were, no doubt, relieved that the demon was stilled and expelled, for the honor of their house of worship. The second miracle was very private, as the Sabbath day was already declining. Consequently, these Sabbath day miracles do not yet provoke any outrage. In Luke 6, however, curing on the Sabbath will become a principal point of controversy. The miracles held important sign value. Sabbath was the day of gathering, when the largest groups of people were assembled. For the miracles to have their intended impact, Sabbath was the best day for them to take place.

And demons also came out of many, crying, "You are the Son of God!" (Luke 4:41a). The demons thought Jesus was a fake, as this chapter began, but after He quiets them down and casts them out, they begin to believe. They do not yet know the full extent of His powers, that He could exorcise the entire world, but they recognize Him faster than the people do. Some people struggle toward faith while others resist, and the demons must be stilled lest they give away the messianic secret. The demons believe in Jesus but will not love Him; the people love Jesus but do not yet believe in Him. *So faith, hope, love abide, these three; but the greatest of these is love* (1 Corinthians 13:13). Head knowledge (wisdom and orthodoxy) and heart knowledge (worship and charity) must unite.

He laid his hands on every one of them and healed them (Luke 4:40b). Jesus is rich in mercy and compassion. He sees the possessed and the sick. Jesus looks past the crowd to see the individual person, who is tormented or hurting. He loves each one.

1. Who led Jesus to the desert? Luke 4:1 Who fills believers? Acts 2:4; 4:31; 6:3; 7:55

2. When does the Church invite you to unite with Jesus in the desert? CCC 540

3. What can you learn from these passages?

Deuteronomy 9:9
1 Kings 19:2–8
Luke 4:1–3

* Recall a time when you fasted for some specific purpose and experienced hunger.

4. Explain tempting God. CCC 2119

Devil Tempts Jesus	Jesus Responds
Luke 4:3	Luke 4:4
Luke 4:7	Luke 4:8
Luke 4:9	Luke 4:12

5. What does Jesus show in overcoming temptation? CCC 539

6. Is the devil real?

Zechariah 3:1–2
1 Peter 5:8–10
1 John 3:8
Revelation 12:9

7. What can you do about the devil? James 4:6–10

8. What will be the devil's final end? Revelation 20:10

9. Does Jesus sympathize with our weakness in temptation?

1 Corinthians 10:13
Hebrews 4:15–16

10. What happened after Jesus overcame temptation?

Luke 4:13
CCC 538

11. Explain the drama in Luke 4:14–24.

12. What can you learn from these verses?

1 Kings 17:1, 8–16
Luke 4:25–26
James 5:17–18

13. Compare these passages.

2 Kings 5:1–14
Luke 4:27

14. How did the people respond to Jesus' preaching in Nazareth? Luke 4:28–30

* Share a time when you responded positively and actively after powerful preaching.

15. Where did Jesus go after leaving Nazareth? Luke 4:31

16. Explain the drama in Luke 4:31–37.

17. How does Jesus exorcise the demon from the man? Luke 4:36

* Do demons still hassle people of God? What can a person do to get free?

18. What did Simon's mother-in-law do after Jesus healed her? Luke 4:38–39

19. What happened following the miracles Jesus performed? Luke 4:40–41

20. Where did Jesus go after preaching, healing, and exorcising? Luke 4:42

** Describe a special, quiet, lonely place in which you pray.

CHAPTER 5

Put Out into the Deep
Luke 5

And when he had ceased speaking, he said to Simon,
"Put out into the deep and let down your nets for a catch."
Luke 5:4

Many Gospel events take place only a few feet from the largest body of fresh water in the Near East, which Luke calls the "Lake of Gennesaret" (Luke 5:1), from the Hebrew *yam-kinneret,* "Harp Sea" (Numbers 34:11; Joshua 12:3, 13:27). Others call it the "Sea of Galilee" (Mark 1:16, 7:31; Matthew 4:18, 15:29; John 6:1) or "Sea of Tiberias" (John 6:1; 21:1), but Luke uses the precise term *limne,* meaning "lake" (Luke 5:1–2; 8:22, 33). The Lake of Gennesaret sits in the Great Rift Valley, a fracture in the planetary crust, where its water surface is seven hundred feet below the level of the Mediterranean. Even so, the lake is very deep, plumbing eighty-four feet on average and one hundred forty-one feet at maximum depth.

Skilled navigators had to read the skies to know whether to put out into those deeps, as capsizing in a storm meant certain death in those waters. Because Jesus trusted Peter's skills, He asked him to do what He knew he could do. Peter knew that Jesus was exceptional; Peter had seen the exorcisms and the healing of his mother-in-law. Jesus had confidence in the skill of Peter, and Peter had trust in the power of Jesus. That was a very good working relationship. Eventually, Peter would be called out over even deeper waters, serving as the first pontiff for forty years, the longest papacy in the history of the Church, which is indeed deep water.

Miraculous draught of fish—*For he was astonished, and all that were with him, at the catch of fish which they had taken* (Luke 5:9). This haul is miraculous not only because of its size, but also because of the time of day. Almighty God put into these fish an instinct to surface by night and dive by day. Tilapia, tristramella, acanthobrama, and other species of fish rise to the surface of the Lake of Gennesaret in the twilight to feed on zooplankton, and dive down at dawn to avoid ultraviolet light. For hundreds and thousands of years these fish have followed this rhythmic feeding cycle, which Peter and the others know very well; they make their living by understanding the behavior patterns of the fish. The strange behavior on this day, when the fish rise to the surface in the morning instead of in the evening, shows that the predictable natural world has bent its rules. That is the miracle—the fish themselves are giving witness to Jesus.

In the thirteenth century, Saint Anthony of Padua went to the town of Rimini to preach along the riverside, but the people refused to come and listen. So Saint Anthony preached to the fish, and they lined up on the banks, thus shaming the people. That Franciscan "miracle of the fish" was a latter-day variant of the Gospel miracle. On both occasions nature responded to the truth before people did.

Duc in Altum!

At the beginning of the new millennium, and at the close of the Great Jubilee during which we celebrated the two thousandth anniversary of the birth of Jesus and a new stage of the Church's journey begins, our hearts ring out with the words of Jesus when one day, after speaking to the crowds from Simon's boat, he invited the Apostle to "put out into the deep" for a catch: *"Duc in altum"* (Luke 5:4). Peter and his first companions trusted Christ's words, and cast the nets. "When they had done this, they caught a great number of fish" (Luke 5:6).

Duc in altum! These words ring out for us today, and they invite us to remember the past with gratitude, to live the present with enthusiasm and to look forward to the future with confidence: "Jesus Christ is the same yesterday and today and for ever" (Hebrews 13:8). . . .

[Our great legacy is] the contemplation of the face of Christ: Christ considered in his historical features and in his mystery, Christ known through his manifold presence in the Church and in the world, and confessed as the meaning of history and the light of life's journey. . . .

The contemplation of Christ's face cannot fail to be inspired by all that we are told about him in Sacred Scripture, which from beginning to end is permeated by his mystery, prefigured in a veiled way in the Old Testament and revealed fully in the New, so that Saint Jerome can vigorously affirm: "Ignorance of the Scriptures is ignorance of Christ." Remaining firmly anchored in Scripture, we open ourselves to the action of the Spirit (cf. John 15:26).

Saint John Paul II, Apostolic Letter At the Beginning of the New Millennium
Novo Millennio Ineunte (January 6, 2001), nos. 1, 15, 17

In order to put out into the deep, Saint John Paul II invites seekers to contemplate the face of Christ in prayer and study. To deepen one's faith, reserve time for prayer, receive the sacraments, especially the Sacraments of Reconciliation and the Holy Eucharist, and ponder God's Word through serious Bible Study. Contemplate the face of Christ. Invite Jesus to transform your life in order to witness to others and become fruitful in evangelism. Saint John Paul II foretold a new springtime of evangelism. Prayer, study, and action can make it unfold.

Jesus heals—*There came a man full of leprosy* (Luke 5:12). In the previous chapter, Jesus reminded the inhabitants of Nazareth that, in the time of the prophet Elisha, God had healed the leper Naaman of Syria. It was prophesied that when the Messiah came, lepers would be healed (Luke 7:22). In due course, one leper (5:12) and, later, the ten lepers appear (17:12). By healing them Jesus restores them to their families. He reaches out to the most marginalized of society, those quarantined because of a contagious disease. Jesus' concern for the sick has become the great tradition of the Church, whose hospitals are among the finest in the world. Saint Damien of Molokai gave his life to bring the sacraments to the leper colony in Hawaii. Saint Aloysius of Gonzaga also sacrificed his life ministering to plague victims in Rome. At his funeral, the rich and the poor alike attended, because illness is no respecter of social rank.

And behold, men were bringing on a bed a man who was paralyzed, and they sought to bring him in and lay him before Jesus (Luke 5:18). The miracle of the fish did not take place on a Sabbath, because Jewish fishermen could not work on Sabbath eve. Traveling on the water was allowed, but working on the water was not. Likewise, the curing of the leper did not take place on a Sabbath, because lepers were not allowed into the synagogues. Jesus certainly met the leper away from the crowds, which absorbed His attention on the Sabbath. Likewise, the healing of the paralytic takes place in a home; the relatives of the sick man would not have dared to loose the tiles of a synagogue. The fish, the leper, and the paralytic have in common that they are working-day miracles, worked not in a holy place but out in the world. In coming chapters, Jesus will work more Sabbath miracles with a result that the sanctimonious will be scandalized. At first, however, Jesus works miracles out in the open, on the lake, in the field, and in the home.

Jesus shows mercy—*Who can forgive sins but God only* (Luke 5:21)? These words come from the mouths of those who do not accept Jesus. Oddly, this same dubious question sometimes issues from Christian mouths today. In this Gospel, Jesus says: *your sins are forgiven* both to the paralytic (Luke 5:20) and to the sinful woman (7:48). In this place, He works the miracle of physical healing so that those present might know that He has the power to forgive sins. Why else did Jesus come but that people might be released from the bondage of sin? Jesus came to forgive sins.

That you may know Jesus has given the Church power to forgive, the Apostle James writes, *Is any among you sick? Let him call for the elders (presbyteroi in Greek, from which we get the word "priest") of the Church, and let them pray over him, anointing him with oil in the name of the Lord; and the prayer of faith will save the sick man, and the Lord will raise him up; and if he has committed sins, he will be forgiven* (James 5:14–15).

After this he went out, and saw a tax collector, named Levi, sitting at the tax office; and he said to him, "Follow me" (Luke 5:27). Jesus calls four fishermen first, but the fifth Apostle called is the tax collector Levi (Luke 5:27–32). Jesus assembles the full complement of twelve Apostles by Luke 6, where Levi is dubbed Matthew (6:15). There may be twelve months, but the number twelve is not just symbolic. It is an organizing principle for Hebrew society. The twelve sons of Jacob fathered the twelve tribes of Israel, all to be ruled by Saul, David, and Solomon. The Essene monks at Qumran had a ruling council of twelve, because they, like Jesus, were serious about the re-establishment of the kingdom.

God created these twelve particular men in this time and place to serve the Messiah with diverse skills. Four Apostles are fishermen (Peter and Andrew, James and John, sons of Zebedee), one a scribe (Levi/Matthew), and another a zealot (Simon). Their native tongue is Aramaic, but one knows the Hebrew language (Peter) and another knows Greek (Philip). God's plan seems to be for each Apostle to serve as a bridge from Jesus to some branch of humanity.

The common impression that the Apostles were unschooled laborers may be mistaken. Those men training to become rabbis were required to learn a trade so they could support their families. Thus, Paul worked as a tentmaker, but no one could accuse him of being uneducated. The tax collector was certainly literate. Andrew was a follower of John the Baptist (John 1:40). Peter had received Jesus in his home (Luke 4:39). John, the beloved disciple, was acquainted with the high priest (John 18:16). How many working class men of the time personally knew John, Jesus, or the high priest? These were young men with connections, but they were also living close to the people.

New wine—*And no one after drinking old wine desires new; for he says, "The old is good"* (Luke 5:39). Jesus gives a series of remarks showing familiarity with the art of winemaking. Desert dwellers do not take alcohol because it causes dehydration, but the Egyptians made beer and the Mediterranean peoples made wine. At Bethsaida, archaeologists found a Rhodian urn, which conveyed Greek wine to the city of Philip, Peter, and Andrew (John 1:44). And Jesus, at the request of His mother Mary, provides excellent new wine for a bride and groom and their guests at the wedding feast at Cana, saving them from embarrassment (John 2).

For the prophets, wine sometimes symbolizes blessings: *And in that day the mountains shall drip sweet wine, and the hills shall flow with milk* (Joel 3:18), and at other times wrath: *you have given us wine to drink that made us reel* (Psalm 60:3), or *take from my hand this cup of the wine of wrath, and make all the nations to whom I send you drink it* (Jeremiah 25:15). The Torah does not forbid alcohol, though some took vows to abstain, like Samson (Judges 13:4ff). By the end of the first century, custom had introduced four cups of wine into the Passover meal, and Jesus offers two to His disciples in the Lucan account of the Last Supper.

Field grapes go through a lengthy metamorphosis before reaching the table, and the aging process is essential to yielding good results. Like aged cheeses, aged wines are best. This saying resembles what the steward said at the wedding in Cana: *Every man serves the good wine first; and when men have drunk freely, then the poor wine; but you have kept the good wine until now* (John 2:10). Jesus demonstrates that He is bringing something new and exceptional to the world that people might not expect.

What is Jesus saying here in this Lucan context? If the saying is applied to Christianity, it means that, concerning this New Way, everything was already present in Judaism, even though some things were hidden and latent. The One who spoke, God the Father, the Word that was spoken, Jesus, and the Spirit that inspired, the Holy Spirit, these

Three were always present. Promises were given that had to ferment in the hearts of those who received them, and the good wine is fulfillment in Christ. Luke quotes this saying because he wants his Jewish readers to know that Jesus came from among them, and he wants his Gentile readers to know that they may claim this Jesus, who was promised from of old.

She Cast Out into the Deep

Rita Antoinette Rizzo was born April 23, 1923 in Ohio. Her parents divorced when she was six, and her mother suffered from depression. She did not have a happy childhood. In fact, her cousins insist that she never had a childhood.

In her teen years, Rita developed severe abdominal pains resulting from serious stomach and intestinal abnormalities. She met a stigmatic, Rhoda Wise, who prayed for her. When she was twenty, after prayer, she went to bed in severe pain and woke up the next morning cured. She had fallen in love with Jesus, who cured her.

Rita entered a cloistered convent, the Adoration Monastery of the Poor Clares of Perpetual Adoration, in Cleveland in 1943, and took the name Sister Angelica. In 1953, while scrubbing the floor, she slipped on the soapy floor and the electric scrubbing machine threw her against a wall, severely injuring her back and legs. After months in a body cast and subsequent surgery, she promised God that if He would allow her to walk again, she would build a monastery in the South.

In 1959, she began making and selling Saint Peter's Fishing Lures by mail order, and later started the Li'l Ole Peanut Company to raise money to build her monastery in Alabama. The Poor Clare Nuns of Perpetual Adoration now live in the magnificent Shrine of the Most Blessed Sacrament in Hanceville, Alabama.

In 1980, Mother Angelica set up a television studio in a garage behind Our Lady of the Angels Monastery in Irondale, Alabama. In 1987, the Eternal Word Television Network (EWTN) started broadcasting the Mass and Catholic television shows twenty-four hours a day. Today, EWTN broadcasts by cable and satellite to 148 million homes in 144 countries and territories around the world. Despite a troubled home life, difficult childhood, many health problems, and limited education, Mother Angelica established an outreach that broadcasts the Good News of Jesus Christ via radio and television all around the world.

1. Describe the drama in Luke 5:1–3.

2. What does Jesus say to Simon? Luke 5:4

3. How does Simon initially respond to Jesus' request? Luke 5:5

4. What is the result of Simon's obedience? Luke 5:6–7

5. What does Peter's response to the miraculous catch of fish signify?

Luke 5:8
CCC 208

6. What does Jesus foretell to Simon? Luke 5:10

* Have you ever felt God ask you to cast out into the deep? Explain.

7. How do Peter, James, and John respond? Luke 5:11

8. What gesture does the leper demonstrate, and what does he ask? Luke 5:12

9. What happens as a result? Luke 5:13–15

10. How does Jesus pray, and for whom does He pray?

Luke 5:16
CCC 2602

* How, where, when, and for whom do you pray?

11. Where can you find the source of the power to heal?

Luke 5:17
CCC 1116

12. Describe the drama in Luke 5:18–19.

13. What does Jesus see in the friends of the paralytic?

Luke 5:20
CCC 26

* Define "faith." CCC 26 Has the faith of another person ever blessed you?

14. Outline the aspects of the miracle and conflict below.

Luke 5:20
Luke 5:21
Luke 5:22–23
Luke 5:24
Luke 5:25

15. How did the onlookers respond to the miracle? Luke 5:26

* Have you ever seen a miracle? Does God work miracles today?

16. How does Levi respond to Jesus' call? Luke 5:28

17. What bothers the Pharisees about Jesus?

Luke 5:29–30
CCC 588

18. Why did Jesus come?

Luke 5:32
1 Timothy 1:15

19. What complaint do the Pharisees make to Jesus? Luke 5:33

20. Explain the parables of Jesus in Luke 5:34–39.

** List some ways you can *put out into the deep*, as Saint John Paul II asked.

Monthly Social Activity

This month, your small group will meet for coffee, tea, or a simple breakfast, lunch, or dessert in someone's home. Pray for this social event and for the host or hostess. Try, if at all possible, to attend.

Share about your favorite childhood hobby or sport. What is your favorite past-time activity now?

Some examples:

— *Coloring or puzzles*

— *Exploring*

— *Tennis*

— *Golf*

— *Traveling*

CHAPTER 6

Lord of the Sabbath
Luke 6

And he said to them,
"The Son of man is lord of the Sabbath."
Luke 6:5

Sabbath law comes directly from God, in the Third Commandment: *Remember the sabbath day, to keep it holy* (Exodus 20:8). Several approaches were proposed in the first century: (1) building a fence around the law so as not to trespass it accidentally; (2) finding practical applications, so that the law could be actually lived out; or (3) living by the heart and spirit of the law. The Pharisees chose the first path. Founders of rabbinic Judaism practiced the second. Jesus and His followers embraced the third. Luke's Jewish readers could see trouble coming already, when Jesus worked His first miracles on a Sabbath (Luke 4). Gentile readers would have been mystified concerning the whole Sabbath question. Roman civil society had no observance of the week. They only had an eight-day business cycle, which had no religious connotations.

Pharisees criticize the disciples, who pick standing grain as they walk through the field on the Sabbath. The Pharisees do not yet attack Jesus personally, but ascribe to Him guilt by association. Jesus does not apologize for the actions of His followers, but instead authoritatively cites a precedent in biblical history, when David's men ate the sacred food set aside for the priests. Jesus then makes a critical Christological statement: *The Son of man is lord of the sabbath* (Luke 6:5; Matthew 12:8; cf. Mark 2:28). The Marcan parallel passage explains this statement: *The sabbath was made for man, not man for the sabbath* (Mark 2:27). God gave this rule for the good of people, so that they could lead happy and healthy lives.

On another Sabbath, when Jesus asks the Pharisees whether it is right to do good or evil, to save a life or destroy it on the Sabbath, they are silent and refuse to answer Him. The miracles should cause awe and conversion, but their hearts are full of darkness and anger. Luke provides five accounts of Jesus' activities on a Sabbath (Luke 4:16–30; 6:1–5; 6–11; 13:10–17; 14:1–6). Jesus demonstrates on those occasions that He is the *lord of the sabbath* (Luke 6:5).

Jesus interprets the Law of Moses for the people and has claimed for Himself the right to interpret that Law. Thus the Messiah, in His humanity, has prudential judgment to apply the divine law. Elsewhere Jesus delegates this messianic authority to Peter: *whatever you bind on earth shall be bound in heaven, and whatever you loose on earth shall be loosed in heaven* (Matthew 16:19b). By virtue of this authority, the early Church transfers the day of worship to Sunday to coincide with the day of Jesus' Resurrection.

Jesus chooses His twelve Apostles—Before making the critical decision of choosing the first bishops for His Church, Jesus spends an entire night in prayer. Simon Peter is listed first among the twelve Apostles, showing his primacy. The Twelve appear to represent ordinary people—rich and poor, working men, some educated, some impulsive, and some zealous. Not a particularly impressive looking group, but after being empowered by the Holy Spirit on Pentecost (Acts 2:1–26), they will boldly proclaim the Gospel throughout the world, and suffer martyrdom for Christ. John, who courageously stood at the foot of the Cross, never abandoning Jesus, was spared a physical martyrdom while suffering a martyrdom of exile.

Luke's list of Apostles ends on a terribly sad and treacherous note, *and Judas Iscariot, who became a traitor* (Luke 6:16b). The Greek word used here for traitor is *prodot s*, an extremely negative term used for someone who betrays his parents, an apostate, or a blasphemer. Luke points out that Judas *became a traitor*. He had free will and a choice, as all people do. People are not born traitors, or liars, or thieves; they become evil from repeating sinful choices. Or, they could repent and be forgiven.

The Beatitudes—Jesus proceeds to address the crowd with authority *on a level place* (Luke 6:17) in the Sermon on the Plain (Luke 6:17–49), which appears very much like a shorter version of Jesus' Sermon on the Mount found in Matthew 5–7. Luke has only four beatitudes, whereas Matthew has eight, but Luke's set is flanked by a corresponding set of four woes. Hebrew literature often lauds what the world grieves, and grieves over what the world considers laudable. Matthew's first beatitude blesses the *poor in spirit* (Matthew 5:3), in line with the prophetic tradition: *But this is the man to whom I will look, he that is humble and contrite in spirit, and trembles at my word* (Isaiah 66:2). Luke's first beatitude blesses those who are materially detached, in line with the wisdom tradition: *Better is a little that the righteous has than the abundance of many wicked* (Psalm 37:16). This beatitude exhorts those who are materially blessed to be generous and to give alms.

> When people desire anything to an excessive degree, they immediately lose their peace of soul. The proud and avaricious are always perturbed, while the humble and the poor in spirit live in peace and contentment.
>
> Thomas a Kempis, *The Imitation of Christ,* 6.1.1

Blessed are you that hunger now, for you shall be satisfied. . . . Woe to you that are full now, for you shall hunger (Luke 6:21a, 25a). Luke's second beatitude corresponds to the fourth in Matthew's set. Again, Matthew spiritualizes his version with the phrase *those who hunger and thirst for righteousness* (Matthew 5:6), in line with the prophetic tradition: *Seek righteousness, seek humility* (Zephaniah 2:3b). Luke's version focuses on bodily hunger, in line with the wisdom writings: *they are not put to shame in evil times, in the days of famine they have abundance* (Psalm 37:19). Again, there is no contradiction between the two accounts, just as there is no conflict between the spiritual and the corporal works of mercy.

Blessed are you that weep now, for you shall laugh. . . . Woe to you that laugh now, for you shall mourn and weep (Luke 6:21b, 25b). Luke's third beatitude corresponds to Matthew's second. After two corporal beatitudes, Luke ascends to the spiritual. Jesus saw people in His crowd dressed in black, grieving lost relatives. Some of the poor wore black rags, while some of the rich were adorned in black finery, because death comes to rich and poor alike. The first beatitude showed how wealth divides people, but this beatitude points out how death unites them. Jesus gave great care to the grieving, and when He conquers death, He gives all who grieve the greatest possible consolation. During His earthly years He delivered from death the only son of the widow of Nain (Luke 7:11–17), the daughter of Jairus, the synagogue official (Luke 8:40–56), and His friend Lazarus (John 11:17–44).

Sermon on the Mount	**Sermon on the Plain**

Blessed are the poor in spirit,
    for theirs is the kingdom of heaven.
Blessed are those who mourn,
    for they shall be comforted.
Blessed are the meek,
    for they shall inherit the earth.
Blessed are those who hunger and thirst
        for righteousness,
    for they shall be satisfied.
Blessed are the merciful,
    for they shall obtain mercy.
Blessed are the pure in heart,
    for they shall see God.
Blessed are the peacemakers,
    for they shall be called sons of God.
Blessed are those who are persecuted
        for righteousness' sake,
    for theirs is the kingdom of heaven.
Blessed are you when men revile you
        and persecute you and utter all
        kinds of evil against you falsely on
        my account.
Rejoice and be glad, for your reward is
    great in heaven, for so men
            persecuted the prophets
            who were before you.
 	
            (Matthew 5:3–11)
	Blessed are you poor,
	    for yours is the kingdom of God.
	Blessed are you that hunger now,
	    for you shall be satisfied.
	Blessed are you that weep now,
	    for you shall laugh.
	Blessed are you when men hate you,
	    and when they exclude and revile you,
	    and cast out your name as evil,
	    on account of the Son of man!
	Rejoice in that day, and leap for joy,
	    for behold,
	        your reward is great in heaven; for
	        so their fathers did to the prophets.
	But woe to you that are rich, for
	    you have received your consolation.
	Woe to you that are full now,
	    for you shall hunger.
	Woe to you that laugh now,
	    for you shall mourn and weep.
	Woe to you, when all men speak well
	    of you, for so their fathers did to the
	    false prophets.
	
	                    (Luke 6:20–26)

Blessed are you when men hate you. . . . Woe to you, when all men speak well of you (Luke 6:22a, 26a). Luke's fourth and last beatitude corresponds to the eighth and last of Matthew. Both sets conclude in the same way, blessing those who are persecuted. Again Matthew focuses on the spiritual aspect with the phrase *for righteousness' sake* (Matthew 5:10), while Luke stresses the corporeal aspect with *on account of the Son of man* (Luke 6:22). The latter term refers to the humanity of the Messiah, and so Luke's version blesses those who suffer in union with the sufferings of Jesus in the flesh.

Do not be troubled by the differences between the two sets of beatitudes. Over the course of His three years of public preaching, Jesus could adapt His material to the needs of a particular audience. The two evangelists clearly concur that the beatitudes were very important in the preaching of Jesus. They stand at the heart of what Pope Emeritus Benedict XVI called "The Torah of the Messiah."

Spiritual interpretation of the beatitudes—Saints Chromatius of Aquileia, Gregory of Nyssa, and Leo the Great plumbed deeper spiritual interpretations of the beatitudes. Rich and poor alike can be either mean or generous. Poverty of spirit requires detachment from material things and attachment to God alone. Materially wealthy people, who love God, recognize with gratitude that everything comes from God, and use their means to help others and advance the Gospel, can be as blessed as a materially poor person who is grateful and willing to share what little he has.

Hunger for righteousness and the desire to grow in union with God surpasses mere longing for bread. *O God, you are my God, I seek you, my soul thirsts for you; my flesh faints for you, as in a dry and weary land where no water is. . . . Because your merciful love is better than life, my lips will praise you. . . . My soul is feasted as with marrow and fat, and my mouth praises you with joyful lips* (Psalm 63:1, 3, 5).

Beyond grieving the death of loved ones, spiritual mourning reflects sincere sorrow for personal sins and the sins of the world, and grief over the ways in which sin wounds others. Most importantly, believers mourn the ways in which sin breaks one's relationship with God. *O LORD, rebuke me not in your anger, nor chasten me in your wrath! . . . There is no soundness in my flesh because of your indignation; there is no health in my bones because of my sin. For my iniquities have gone over my head; they weigh like a burden too heavy for me* (Psalm 38:1, 3–4).

The beatitudes provide steppingstones for each disciple, rich or poor, to grow in virtue and holiness. Each Christian must strive for detachment from inordinate desires, and become attached to God alone. Everyone hungers and thirsts for a relationship with God. On the path to holiness, love and trust God, express gratitude to God for His blessings, confess and show remorse for sin, and demonstrate a willingness to show God's mercy and forgiveness to others.

But I say to you that hear, Love your enemies, do good to those who hate you (Luke 6:27). The Sermon on the Plain skips over two parables and several paragraphs of commentary on murder, adultery, and divorce, and rejoins Matthew after his quotation of the talonic law: *An eye for an eye and a tooth for a tooth* (Matthew 5:38; cf. Exodus 21:23–24; Leviticus 24:19–20; Deuteronomy 19:21). The Torah of Moses ensured that no more would be exacted than was required in strict justice; hence the rule was *a life* (only) *for a life*. The Torah of the Messiah, however, seeks to break the vicious cycle of violence by foregoing just punishments.

Matthew's Sermon on the Mount has one hundred nine verses, and Luke's Sermon on the Plain has only thirty-three verses. About half of the seventy-six missing verses appear elsewhere in Luke. So textual differences are real, but do not alter the thrust of the teaching. Both sermons make equal sense coming from the mouth of the Master Himself. One of the characteristics of Luke as a writer is that he preserves the textual integrity and authentic voice of his sources.

Be merciful, even as your Father is merciful (Luke 6:36). This little verse is the only sermon material that Luke provides, which Matthew does not. It smoothly fits the material before and after, and seems to be an integral part of the text, not exhibiting the character of a gloss. This statement resembles the verse, *Be perfect, as your heavenly Father is perfect* (Matthew 5:48), from earlier in the Sermon on the Mount. Luke's version is less likely to make the scrupulous reader get tied up in knots. Since God is perfect in mercy, the two verses actually have one and the same meaning. If one cannot be perfect in everything, since humans are not God, then one should strive at least to be more and more perfect in mercy, and hopefully that should be more than good enough to please God.

Judge not, and you will not be judged (Luke 6:37)—People who desire to rationalize objectively sinful behavior frequently quote this verse. But, Luke later reports Jesus saying, *And why do you not judge for yourselves what is right* (Luke 12:57)? Jesus also says: *Do not judge by appearances, but judge with right judgment* (John 7:24). Truthfully, every single day, each person must make many judgments—that this is good or bad, to do this or that, to speak or to keep silent. The Greek word that Luke uses in Luke 6:37 is *katadikaz* , a strong word that denotes condemnation. A parent judges that lying or stealing cannot be tolerated in a child and must be punished, without denouncing or condemning the child. And the Church must also exercise judgment in punishing cases of grievous sin within the Church.

Every one who comes to me and hears my words and does them, I will show you what he is like: he is like a man building a house, who dug deep, and laid the foundation upon rock (Luke 6:47–48a). The Sermon on the Plain concludes (Luke 6:47–49) with the same double parable that also concludes the Sermon on the Mount (Matthew 7:24–27). These two parables form a framing device that Jesus commonly used in His preaching. They serve magnificently for the purpose, because the Lord of the Sabbath commands that His preaching be put into practice. The teaching is meant to move the hearer to action, upon a rock-solid basis. And, as Saint Paul explains, that rock is Christ (1 Corinthians 10:4). Build your faith on Jesus the rock.

1. How does Jesus respond to the Pharisees' criticism of violating the Sabbath?

1 Samuel 21:1–6
Luke 6:3–5
CCC 581–582

2. Explain the drama in Luke 6:6–11.

3. What rhetorical, logical question does Jesus ask the Pharisees? Luke 6:9

4. How long does Jesus pray, prior to choosing His Apostles? Luke 6:12

* How long do you think a Christian should spend in prayer each day?

5. Who did Jesus choose as Apostles, and who are their successors?

Luke 6:13–16
CCC 1555–1556

6. Why did crowds follow Jesus? What did they try to do?

Luke 6:17–19
CCC 1504

7. Explain some blessings and expected outcomes.

Luke 6:20
CCC 2444
Luke 6:21a
Luke 6:21b
Luke 6:22–23

8. Explain the woes and their outcomes.

Luke 6:24
CCC 2445
Luke 6:25a
Luke 6:25b
Luke 6:26

9. What do the beatitudes reveal? CCC 2546

10. What can you learn from the passages below?

Luke 6:27–30
Romans 12:17

11. Explain the "Golden Rule." Luke 6:31

12. Explain the challenge in Luke 6:35.

13. Find a practical application in the following.

Luke 6:36
CCC 1458
CCC 2842

* Does frequent confession help one to be merciful? When was your last confession?

14. What can you know about making judgments?

Luke 6:36
John 7:24

* Are you more inclined to judge quickly, or to be silent when you should correct?

15. Why should one be generous? Luke 6:38

16. What must one do before correcting another? Luke 6:39–42

17. Where do good and evil originate? Luke 6:43–45

18. How can you protect the springs of life? Proverbs 4:23

19. What is Jesus' warning in Luke 6:46, 49?

20. How should a person respond to Jesus' words? Luke 6:47–48

Chapter 7

Faith and Humility
Luke 7

Lord, do not trouble yourself,
for I am not worthy to have you come under my roof;
therefore I did not presume to come to you.
But say the word, and let my servant be healed.
Luke 7:6b–7

A humble centurion asks Jesus to heal his servant—The centurion, a professional military officer in charge of one hundred men, understands authority. Even today, a person who manages a hundred workers has significant responsibility. Despite first century cultural norms, which allowed treating slaves inhumanely, this centurion recognizes the dignity of the human person and does not treat his servant as a thing to be used or abused and then tossed away. Interestingly, the Jewish townspeople of Capernaum intercede on behalf of the centurion, saying: *He is worthy to have you do this for him, for he loves our nation, and he built us our synagogue* (Luke 7:4). The centurion has servants and considerable wealth. He shows generosity to the people of the town, whose faith he does not even share, by building them a synagogue in which they can worship their God!

Jesus goes to the centurion, but before He arrives, the centurion sends friends to intercept Jesus. The centurion knows that entering the home of a Gentile will probably make Jesus ritually impure. Note the generosity and humility of this man. The centurion knows he is unworthy. The Church employs the words of the centurion in the Eucharistic liturgy before receiving Holy Communion, "Lord, I am not worthy that you should enter under my roof, but only say the word and my soul shall be healed." This centurion is the first Gentile in Luke's Gospel to come to faith in the power of Jesus' word, and Jesus marvels at the man's faith.

Luke shows that even unclean Gentiles can accept Jesus and His message in faith. Later, Luke provides a parallel account in Acts 10 with the first Gentile convert in the early Church, the centurion Cornelius, *a devout man who feared God with all his household, gave alms liberally to the people, and prayed constantly to God* (Acts 10:2). Simon Peter recognizes faith in Cornelius, and preaches the Gospel to him and his entire household. These accounts of the Gentiles' profound faith in Jesus contrast with the lack of faith and hostility of those religious leaders who saw the works Jesus did and should have believed in Him, but refused.

Jesus restores to life the dead son of the widow of Nain—Nain, in Jesus' time was a prosperous village southeast of Nazareth on the way to Mount Tabor, near Samaria and Judea. As Jesus passes thriving olive and fig orchards, He meets the funeral procession of a stranger and encounters a widow weeping over the dead body of her only son. Jesus shows compassion for the suffering of others. The condition of widows in Jesus' time was pitiful: widows could not inherit their deceased husband's property, and were totally dependent on the charity of relatives for their very subsistence. Widows were defenseless and hopeless. No grief is greater than a parent mourning the death of a child. Jesus shows tenderness and compassion. Jesus tells the widow: *Do not weep* (Luke 7:13). Then, He makes Himself ritually impure by touching the bier of the corpse, and says, *Young man, I say to you, arise* (Luke 7:14). The dead man obeys. Jesus raises the dead!

And he gave him to his mother (Luke 7:15). The Prophet Elijah utters these same words when he restores life to the dead son of the widow of Zarephath, *and delivered him to his mother* (1 Kings 17:23). When Elijah delivered the dead boy to his mother, the woman said, *"Now I know that you are a man of God, and that the word of the* LORD *in your mouth is truth"* (1 Kings 17:24). If the widow of Zarepath could recognize the power of God at work, and the people of Nain could come to fear and glorify God, what prevents others from coming to faith in Jesus?

John the Baptist sends messengers to Jesus—When Jesus spoke in the Nazareth synagogue, He opened the scroll of the prophet Isaiah and read, *The Spirit of the Lord is upon me, because he has anointed me to preach good news to the poor. He has sent me to proclaim <u>release to the captives</u>* (Luke 4:18). Now, Jesus sends word back to John, quoting Isaiah, in recounting His deeds: *the blind receive their sight, the lame walk, lepers are cleansed, and the deaf hear, the dead are raised up* (Luke 7:22). But, Jesus does not say anything about releasing captives from prison. John the Baptist knows that Jesus has the power to free him from captivity. Why doesn't Jesus set John free? Later, Luke reports that an angel releases Peter from prison (Acts 5:19). But, Jesus does only the will of His Father. John must trust God, without understanding.

Jesus praises John the Baptist. *I tell you, among those born of women none is greater than John* (Luke 7:28). John the Baptist demonstrates model discipleship. John comes onto the scene, does his job, and then leaves. John does not wait around for accolades or applause. He just does what God has appointed him to do, and he does it well. Jesus chastises the people for not believing John and repenting. John fasts and Jesus feasts, and the people criticize both of them. They are like spoiled, lazy children who complain that they have nothing to do and are bored, but stubbornly refuse to go outside and play the games that the other children are playing.

Wisdom is justified by all her children (Luke 7:35), explains Jesus. In the Wisdom literature of the Bible, Lady Wisdom is portrayed as a manifestation of God giving gifts to those who seek after them. *Wisdom, the fashioner of all things, taught me. For in her there is a spirit that is intelligent, holy . . . all-powerful, overseeing all, and penetrating through all spirits. . . . She is a breath of the power of God* (Wisdom 7:22, 25). *The fear of the* LORD *is the beginning of wisdom, and the knowledge of the Holy One is insight* (Proverbs 9:10). Jesus illustrates how unwise it is to ignore and criticize the ways of Almighty God. Trusting God shows true wisdom.

Jesus forgives a sinful woman—Jesus accepts a dinner invitation at the home of Simon, a Pharisee. In all cultures, to invite someone to one's home for a meal indicates honor, respect, and hospitality. Hosts make special preparations and provide a warm welcome to guests. Today, hosts shake hands and take coats. If guests come from afar, freshening up in a restroom is offered. In the Holy Land of Jesus' time, hosts embraced guests with a kiss, provided water for washing dirty feet, and offered some fragrant oil. None of these courtesies were offered to Jesus, by the host or his servants. But a notoriously sinful woman will come and make up for what is lacking in Simon the Pharisee.

In antiquity, people reclined on cushions around a table and shared food placed in the center. Chairs were uncommon. People often took food with their hands, or used bread to scoop up the food. Dining in this fashion made hygiene rather important. A guest would like to avoid smelling badly in close proximity to his dinner companions. Foot washing and aromatic oils became highly desirable for everyone at the table. But Jesus is led to the table, unwashed and un-anointed.

A sinful woman of the city somehow gets admittance into the Pharisee's home, and begins weeping for her sins. She bathes and kisses the feet of Jesus and anoints them with costly ointment. This woman models a truly repentant soul, who loves Jesus. Nothing in the text says that the woman is a prostitute, but being a woman of the city and a notorious sinner leads one to infer that her sins were very public. Prostitutes solicit customers in public. Some sins are committed in private where only God sees them. But whatever her sins may have been, everybody knew about them. Simon the Pharisee and his other guests know this woman. She has not sinned in secret and she has not sinned alone. Some sins make the front page and everyone sees them.

> You have been at some pains throughout to accuse yourself of a multitude of sins. But I know that you love the Almighty Lord fervently, and I trust in His mercy that the sentence pronounced in regard to a certain holy woman proceeds from the mouth of Truth in your regard also: "Her sins, though they are many, are forgiven her, because she has loved much."
>
> Saint Gregory the Great (540–604), *Letter to Gregoria*, 7, 22

Simon the Pharisee mutters under his breath, and Jesus hears him. Beware of sinful thoughts entertained in silence! Jesus knows the hearts and thoughts of people. Simon judges both the sinful woman and Jesus. *If this man were a prophet, he would have known who and what sort of woman this is who is touching him, for she is a sinner* (Luke 7:39). Newsflash! Simon, we are *all* sinners! Who said this man is a prophet? The people of Nain, who saw Jesus raise the dead son of the widow, *glorified God, saying, "A great prophet has arisen among us!" and "God has visited his people"* (Luke 7:16). Simon makes a big mistake in judging Jesus and also in judging the sinful woman. Time will tell, and God will judge. Simon can see the woman's sin, but he is blind to his own sin.

The essence of Christian perfection consists in union with God by charity. While charity, by conforming our wills to God's, unites us to Him, grave sin, which directly opposes His will, produces the opposite effect. In other words, charity is the force uniting man to God, and sin the force drawing him away. Serious sin is therefore the greatest enemy of the spiritual life, since it not only injures it, but destroys it in its constituent elements: charity and grace. This destruction, this spiritual death, is the inevitable result of sin, the act by which man voluntarily detaches himself from God, the source of life, charity and grace.

Father Gabriel of Saint Mary Magdalene, OCD, *Divine Intimacy*
(London: Baronius Press, 2008), 284

When Jesus tells Simon that He has something to say to him, Simon asks: *What is it, Teacher?* (Luke 7:40). Luke uses the Greek word *didaskale* for teacher thirteen times in his Gospel (7:40; 8:49; 9:38; 10:25; 11:45; 12:13; 18:18; 19:39; 20:21, 28, 39; 21:7; 22:11). The Teacher prepares to give Simon a lesson that he will not want to hear, and may or may not learn. Jesus tells a story of a creditor with two debtors, whose debts are forgiven. One owes a small debt and the other owes an impossibly enormous amount. Similar to Socrates, Jesus draws Simon into the discussion by asking him a question. Simon gives the correct answer—the person who is forgiven more will love more. Simon passes the test, but flunks the class. If you get Jesus wrong, you fail at life and endanger your eternal destiny. Simon fails to correctly identify the Divine Teacher reclining at his table. Divine Mercy speaks to Simon, but Simon is too proud to listen and respond.

Simon indicts himself, as Jesus describes the loving gestures that the sinful woman has given to Jesus, in contrast to the lack of love and hospitality that Simon has shown. *And he said to her, "Your sins are forgiven"* (Luke 7:48). Those at table, friends of Simon, probably other Pharisees murmur among themselves. *Who is this, who even forgives sins* (Luke 7:49)? This is an excellent question, and they all know the answer—only God has the power to forgive sins. So, who can this be? Luke 7 opens with a humble, generous centurion who recognizes Jesus' power and authority. Jesus marvels at the faith of that centurion. Luke 7 ends with Jesus recognizing the faith and charity of a notoriously sinful woman, who repents of her sins and loves Jesus. *And he said to the woman, "Your faith has saved you; go in peace"* (Luke 7:50). Pride proves a major obstacle to faith. Humility and charity are virtues that predispose one to accept Jesus and grow in faith.

All of these signs and miracles have Christological significance, and the scribes and Pharisees know it. Only God has the power to forgive sins. God alone has the power to heal people of incurable illnesses. Only God has the power to release the captives. God alone has the power to restore a dead person to life. The prophets foretold that the "anointed one" would heal the sick and set captives free. Jesus of Nazareth does all of these things. Jesus works signs and miracles. So, who could Jesus be? Jesus is the Messiah, the Anointed One of God! Isn't this obvious?

> *The end of all things is at hand; therefore keep sane and sober for your prayers. Above all hold unfailing your love for one another, since love covers a multitude of sins. Practice hospitality ungrudgingly to one another. As each has received a gift, employ it for one another, as good stewards of God's varied grace* (1 Peter 4:7–10).

1. Why did the elders of the Jews say the centurion was worthy? Luke 7:1–5

2. How does Jesus respond to need? Luke 7:6

3. What message does the centurion send to Jesus? Luke 7:6–8

4. What virtue does the centurion display? When do you pray thus? Luke 7:6b

5. Use a dictionary or the CCC Glossary to define the virtue of humility.

6. How can you grow in this virtue of humility? CCC 2559

* Identify three contemporary famous people or friends who are humble.

7. How does Jesus judge the centurion, and what does He do? Luke 7:9–10

8. Compare the passages below.

1 Kings 17:17–24
2 Kings 4:32–37
Luke 7:11–15

9. What does Jesus show in this miracle?

CCC 994
CCC 1503
CCC 547, 549

10. How did the common people respond to this miracle? Luke 7:16

11. What can you learn about John the Baptist?

CCC 718
CCC 719

12. What does John ask his disciples to ask Jesus? Luke 7:18–20

13. How does Jesus answer them? Luke 7:21–23

14. What does Jesus teach the crowds about John the Baptist?

Luke 7:24–27
Luke 7:28
Luke 7:31–32
Luke 7:33–34

15. What can you learn about wisdom?

Luke 7:35
Sirach 1:1, 5
Sirach 1:26
Wisdom 7:22ff

16. Explain the drama in Luke 7:36–50.

17. What does Simon say to himself? Luke 7:39

18. Explain the forgiveness of sins.

Luke 7:47–49
CCC 588
CCC 1441

19. Find an example of Jesus hearing a prayer said in silence.

Luke 7:37–39
CCC 2616

20. List the truths in the following passages.

Luke 7:48–49
Luke 7:50

* What one thing could you do to grow in humility or increase your faith?

Chapter 8

Women
Luke 8

Soon afterward he went on through cities and villages,
preaching and bringing the good news of the kingdom of God.
And the Twelve were with him, and also some women
who had been healed of evil spirits and infirmities:
Mary, called Magdalene, from whom seven demons had gone out,
and Joanna, the wife of Chuza, Herod's steward, and Susanna,
and many others, who provided for them out of their means.
Luke 8:1–3

Women open Luke 8 and appear throughout the chapter. Note the visit from Mary, the mother of Jesus, the healing of a hemorrhaging woman who had suffered for twelve years, and the restoration to life of a dead twelve-year-old girl, the only child of her parents. Among the evangelists, Luke is distinctive in the importance that he gives to women. While it was not unusual for women in Jesus' time to support rabbis and religious leaders with their money, it was unique for women to follow Jesus, along with His disciples. The Church mirrors Jesus in accepting men and women, rich and poor, old and young, single and married, healthy and sick, sinners and saints. Look at the Catholic Church—here comes everybody! Saint Pope John Paul II encouraged women in his encyclical *Mulieris Dignitatum*.

On the Dignity and Vocation of Women

"He who is mighty has done great things for me" (Luke 1:49). These words certainly refer to the conception of her Son, who is the "Son of the Most High" (Luke 1:32), the "holy one" of God; but they can also signify *the discovery of her own feminine humanity*. He *"has done great things for me"*: this is the discovery *of all the richness and personal resources of femininity*, all the eternal originality of the "woman," just as God wanted her to be, a person for her own sake, who discovers herself "by means of a sincere gift of self. . . ."

A woman's dignity is closely connected with the love which she receives by the very reason of her femininity; it is likewise connected *with the love which she gives in return*. The truth about the person and about love is thus confirmed. With regard to the truth about the person, we must turn again to the Second Vatican Council: "Man, who is the only creature on earth that God willed for its own sake, cannot fully find himself except through a sincere gift of self. . . ." *Woman can only find herself by giving love to others*.

Saint John Paul II, On the Dignity and Vocation of Women
Mulieris Dignitatem (August 15, 1988), nos. 11, 30

Luke introduces Mary Magdalene, who had been delivered of seven demons, Joanna, the wife of Chuza, Herod's steward, who was obviously a woman of means and prominence, Susanna, and others who support Jesus with their means and follow Him. Some of these same women remain faithful to Jesus all the way to Golgotha and do not abandon Him as most of the Apostles do. And on Easter Sunday morning, Luke reports that it was *Mary Magdalene and Joanna and Mary the mother of James and the other women with them who told this [that Jesus was no longer in the tomb] to the apostles* (Luke 24:10). At the beginning of the Gospel of Luke, the Archangel Gabriel appears to a young woman in Nazareth. And women continue to appear throughout Luke's Gospel and remain to the very end.

When the Virgin Mary and some relatives come to see Jesus but fail to reach Him because of the crowd, Jesus says, *My mother and my brethren are those who hear the word of God and do it* (Luke 8:21). On first glance, this could appear insulting to the Mother of God. However, some Jews were filled with pride in their race as sons of Abraham. Jesus shows that faith matters more than bloodlines. Mary is more blessed because she trusted the word of God and obeyed.

Parables—Jesus offers many parables, which explain theological truths in very common, everyday terms. Farming, seeds, lamps, and light are familiar to people everywhere in all times. After Jesus gives the parable of the sower, He later explains it clearly for His disciples. Luke includes more parables than any other evangelist.

> **Parable**—a short story
> based on a common, familiar life experience,
> used to teach a moral lesson,
> and demanding a decision or response.

Jesus conquers nature—Exhausted from walking, preaching, teaching, and healing people, Jesus falls asleep in a boat. The Sea of Galilee frequently experiences sudden, violent storms with huge squalls of wind and sea spray. The Apostles understand the weather and have experienced many of these storms, but they are terrified and wake Jesus. *Master [epistata in Greek], Master, we are perishing!* (Luke 8:24). In the Old Testament, storms at sea symbolize danger and chaos. During the Exodus, the Red Sea formed a barrier to the Promised Land. *He rebuked the Red Sea, and it became dry; and he led them through the deep as through a desert* (Psalm 106:9). The Psalmist foretells: *Then they cried to the LORD in their trouble, and he delivered them from their distress; he made the storm be still, and the waves of the sea were hushed* (Psalm 107:28–29).

When Jesus wakes up and rebukes the wind and the waves, the seas calm. He chastises the disciples for their lack of faith. The disciples are afraid and marvel, and ask: *Who then is this, that he commands even wind and water, and they obey him* (Luke 8:25)? Earlier, when Jesus healed a paralytic, a similar question was asked: *Who is this?* (5:21). And when Jesus forgave the sins of the sinful woman in Simon's house, the guests asked: *Who is this, who even forgives sins?* (7:49). This becomes the sixty-four million dollar question that challenges every human being. Who is Jesus? How would you answer? What evidence can you find? What response must follow the correct answer to that question?

Jesus drives out demons—After Jesus overcomes the forces of nature in calming the storm at sea, He enters the area of Gerasa, one of the Gentile cities of the Decapolis, and faces satanic, spiritual forces. The plight of the demoniac is grave. He is naked, living away from family and friends in a graveyard, tormented, often shackled. The forces of evil constantly try to destroy people. The Gerasene demoniac illustrates how diabolic forces assault and torment people. Jesus wants to save people. Satan wants to annihilate people. The spiritual battle between good and evil rages on.

The demoniac recognizes Jesus and falls down before Him. *What have you to do with me, Jesus, Son of the Most High God? I beg you, do not torment me* (Luke 8:28). Interestingly, all along, people have been asking the question, "Who is this?" And yet, the demons know clearly who Jesus is. The tormenter begs Jesus, the healer and deliverer, not to torment him. Jesus demands that the demon reveal his name. In ancient cultures, to know a person's name means to have power over him, and to have some control over his destiny. The demon reveals his name: Legion. A legion consisted of six thousand foot soldiers. This poor man is infested with evil. But Jesus has ultimate power over evil. He exorcizes the man, who returns to the feet of Jesus, clothed and in his right mind, begging to follow Jesus. But Jesus sends the man back to his home, to witness to others what God has done for him.

Miracles for a woman and a girl—Jesus returns to Capernaum and a crowd welcomes Him. Up to this point, Luke has been very critical of the Jewish leaders. But in Capernaum, Luke introduces Jairus, a leader of the synagogue who falls at Jesus' feet, begging Him to come to his house and heal his only child, a twelve-year-old daughter who is dying. Jesus responds immediately to the man's need. But on the way to the house of Jairus, something extraordinary happens.

A woman, who has been bleeding for as long as Jairus' daughter has been alive, reaches out to touch the tassel (*kraspedos* in Greek) of Jesus' cloak (*himation* in Greek). Two things can be gleaned from this information: (1) Jesus was an observant Jew who wore a prayer shawl, and a cloak with prayer fringes, reminders to pray; (2) the suffering woman is humble and desperate. She is ritually impure and does not want to make Jesus also ritually impure by touching Him. This woman demonstrates such amazing faith in that she knows if she can only touch the hem of Jesus' garment, she will be healed. Jesus asks, *Who was it that touched me?* (Luke 8:45). Peter is incredulous. They are in a huge crowd. People are pushing and shoving. Everyone wants to see Jesus. Everyone tries to touch Jesus.

When all denied it, Peter said, "Master [epistata in Greek], the multitudes surround you and press upon you!" (Luke 8:45b). But Jesus knows that someone has touched Him, for He feels power going forth from Him. The woman comes to Jesus trembling, and falls down before Him—a perfect posture before the King of kings, the Divine Healer. She admits that she has touched Jesus' cloak and has been immediately healed. Perhaps she expects to be chastised. But Jesus speaks tenderly to her, *Daughter, your faith has made you well; go in peace* (Luke 8:48).

An amazing lesson hides in this story. You may feel trapped in the crowd. You may be sick and tired of feeling sick and tired. You may feel that God has forgotten you, or passed you by. And yet, the desperate woman teaches us to reach out to Jesus anyway. Even if you feel that Jesus is busy with other, more urgent matters, Christ is the source of God's healing power. The woman was healed while Jesus was walking away. Jesus did not touch her, nor speak to her, nor do anything. Yet, divine power reached into the broken places of the bleeding woman and healed her.

Meanwhile, a servant comes from Jairus' house to announce that the little girl is dead. Now, skeptics might suggest that the girl was only swooning or in a coma. But death was not hidden in the first century as it is today. People slaughtered their lambs and drained the blood. Meat did not come in plastic wrapped packages. Elderly loved ones died at home in their beds, not in nursing homes or hospitals. People in Capernaum understood death much better than we do today. They saw death up close, all the time. Jesus does not deny that the girl is dead. Jesus knows she is dead. But, He instructs Jairus not to fear, only to believe, and she will be well.

Jesus encounters two occasions to become ritually impure. Leviticus 15:19ff forbids touching a woman who has a discharge of blood. Everything that touches her becomes unclean. Leviticus 21:11ff decrees that touching a dead body makes one ritually impure. According to Mosaic Law, a faithful Jew should not touch a person who is bleeding or has a discharge, nor touch a corpse. But Jesus shows mercy and compassion to hurting people.

Only five people are permitted to enter the dead girl's room with Jesus—Peter, James, John, Jairus, and his wife. Jesus takes the little dead girl by the hand and commands her to rise. Her spirit returns to her and she gets up at once. And then, Jesus tells her parents to get her something to eat! Oh, the beautiful details that Luke recounts for readers! Luke recounts two times that Jesus raises an only child from death in parallel passages. In Luke 7:11–17, Jesus brings back to life the dead only son of the widow of Nain. Here, in Luke 8:40–56, Jesus restores to life the deceased only child of Jairus, the synagogue ruler. A twelve-year-old girl lives, and a woman recovers from a twelve-year illness. Faith in God—trust in Jesus—produces miracles in the lives of men, women, and children.

Who is this? Jesus of Nazareth, the King of kings, and Lord of lords, the Teacher, the Master, who winds and sea obey, who demons fear, who conquers death and disease and darkness. Jesus is the miracle worker who gives new life to men, women, and children. Jesus invites everyone to come to Him—men and women, rich and poor, young and old, healthy and ill, sinner and saint—all come to Jesus for mercy.

A Woman of Faith

Gianna Francesca Beretta was born in Magenta, Italy on October 4, 1922, into a large, devout, Catholic family. She completed medical school in Milan in 1949, and began practicing pediatric medicine. Gianna hoped to join her brother, a missionary priest in Brazil, to provide medical care for poor women and children. However, God had other plans for her.

In December 1954, Gianna met Pietro Molla, an engineer, who was ten years her senior. They fell in love and married in September 1955. In their marriage, despite two miscarriages, Gianna and Pietro were blessed with three healthy children, a son, Pierluigi, and two daughters, Maria Zita and Laura.

Gianna was pregnant with her fourth child in 1961 when doctors discovered a mass on her uterus early in her pregnancy. They proposed three options for her to consider: (1) an abortion, which would save her life and allow her to possibly have future pregnancies, but terminate the life of her unborn child; (2) a hysterectomy, which would preserve her life, but take the life of the child, and remove all possibility of future pregnancies; or (3) surgical removal of the tumor only, which might or might not be successful. Gianna and Pietro rejected the first two options, which would have destroyed their child, and elected the third choice.

Complications developed and persisted throughout her pregnancy. Doctor Gianna understood exactly what was happening to her and put her trust in God. She was clear and firm to her family and her doctors in expressing her desires. Gianna said, "This time it will be a difficult delivery, and they may have to save one or the other—I want them to save my baby."

On Good Friday, April 21, 1962, Gianna Emanuela Molla, a healthy baby girl, was successfully delivered via Caesarean section. She would grow into a strong Catholic woman and physician, like her mother. However, her mother died a few days later.

Along with her father and siblings, Gianna was present in Rome on May 16, 2004, when Saint John Paul II canonized her mother. In his homily at her canonization Mass, Saint John Paul II said that, "Gianna is a simple, but more than ever, significant messenger of divine love."

Women in the Bible followed Jesus, supported Him, and were faithful to Him. Today, women in the Church continue to follow Jesus and to trust God, even in the most difficult circumstances of life. Saint Gianna Molla provides a contemporary example of heroic self-sacrifice. She is a patron saint for mothers, unborn children, women desiring children or needing help in pregnancy, and physicians. Her beautiful prayer is suitable for men, women, and children to pray.

1. Explain something about the women who followed Jesus. Luke 8:1–3

Mary Magdalene
Joanna
Susanna

2. Where else can you find women disciples?

Matthew 27:55–56
Mark 15:40
Luke 23:49, 55
John 19:25

3. What can you learn about man and woman in God's plan?

CCC 371	
CCC 372	
CCC 373	
CCC 378	

* Give evidence that the Catholic Church is pro-woman, pro-man, and pro-child.

4. Use a dictionary to define the word "parable."

5. How does Jesus use parables? CCC 546

6. How and when do you *hear the word of God?* (Luke 8:11, 15)

7. Explain the parable of the sower. Luke 8:4–15

Seed	
Seeds along the path	
Seeds on rocky ground	
Seeds among thorns	
Good Soil	

8. What can you learn from the following verses?

Luke 8:17	
Ephesians 5:11–14	

9. How does the Blessed Mother exemplify faith in the following passages?

Luke 1:38	
Luke 8:21	
CCC 148	
CCC 149	

* What kind of soil are you in? What kind of fruit are you bearing just now?

10. Outline the storm at sea.

Luke 8:22	
Luke 8:23	
Luke 8:24	
Luke 8:25	

* Have you even encountered any storms in the sea of your life? Did you trust God?

11. What do the Psalms say about the sea?

Psalm 78:13, 53	
Psalm 107:28–31	

12. How does the demon-possessed man address Jesus? Luke 8:28

13. What does Jesus' exorcism indicate? CCC 550

14. What happened to the man after he was delivered? Luke 8:38–39

15. What story is entwined in the raising of Jairus' daughter? Luke 8:43–48

16. What restrictions were placed on a bleeding Jewish woman? Leviticus 15:19–27

17. What does Jesus say when learning of the death of the child? Luke 8:50

18. Who was present with Jesus in Jairus' house? Luke 8:51

19. What evidence can you find that the child was actually dead? Luke 8:49, 53

20. What interesting thing does Jesus ask them to do? Luke 8:55

* List your three favorite women saints, and three contemporary holy women.

CHAPTER 9

The Christ of God
Luke 9

"But who do you say that I am?"
And Peter answered, "The Christ of God."
Luke 9:20

The mission of the Apostles—Jesus gave the twelve Apostles spiritual power and authority over demons and disease. He then sent them out to preach the kingdom of God, to heal, and to deliver the oppressed from demonic influences. The Twelve were to take nothing with them, but were to rely entirely on God to provide for their sustenance. The Apostles obeyed Jesus. They went through towns and villages preaching the Good News and healing people, just as their Master had done.

Throughout Luke's Gospel, people have been asking the question: *Who is this?* Now even Herod Antipas, (the son of Herod the Great who had ordered the slaughter of the innocents after Jesus' birth), asks this important question. Curiosity can lead one to faith, but can also just remain idle curiosity. Herod asks, *"Who is this about whom I hear such things?" And he [Herod] sought to see him [Jesus]* (Luke 9:9). Eventually, Herod does see Jesus (23:6–12), but it does him no good. Instead of putting his faith in Jesus, repenting of his sins, and begging God's mercy, Herod treats Jesus with mockery and contempt.

Bread for the hungry—The only miracle reported by all four of the evangelists in their Gospels is Jesus' multiplication of five loaves and two fish to feed the five thousand (Matthew 14:13–21; Mark 6:32–44; Luke 9:12–17; John 6:1–15). Luke matches the verbs in the parallel passages of the feeding of the five thousand (Luke 9:16), the institution of the Eucharist at the Last Supper (22:19), and the breaking of bread at Emmaus (24:30). Jesus takes, blesses, breaks, and gives the bread.

Feeding the Multitude	Last Supper	Emmaus Supper
Taking the five loaves and two fish he looked up to heaven, and blessed and broke them, and gave them (Luke 9:16).	*He took bread, and when he had given thanks he broke it and gave it to them* (Luke 22:19).	*He took the bread and blessed and broke it, and gave it to them* (Luke 24:30).

Matthew reports that when Jesus saw the hungry crowds, *he had compassion for them, because they were harassed and helpless, like sheep without a shepherd* (Matthew 9:36). Luke presents the preaching of the Gospel (Luke 9:6) just prior to the feeding of the five thousand (Luke 9:13–16). The Catholic Mass follows this same pattern. The Liturgy of the Word immediately precedes the Liturgy of the Eucharist. The feeding of the five thousand in Luke's Gospel immediately precedes Jesus foretelling His Passion, death and Resurrection, and His invitation to discipleship—to take up one's cross and follow Him. The celebration of the Eucharist provides an opportunity for table fellowship, while also making present the redemptive sacrifice of Jesus on the Cross. Saint Paul says, *for as often as you eat this bread and drink the chalice, you proclaim the Lord's death until he comes* (1 Corinthians 11:26). Receive the Eucharist worthily and frequently.

The Christ of God—Luke's Gospel has been repeating the question, *Who is this?* (Luke 5:21; 7:49; 8:25). Now, Jesus poses this same question to the disciples. *"But who do you say that I am?" And Peter answered, "The Christ of God"* (Luke 9:20). Matthew reveals the source of Peter's wisdom. *Jesus answered him, "Blessed are you, Simon Bar-Jona! For flesh and blood has not revealed this to you, but my Father who is in heaven"* (Matthew 16:17). Peter gives the correct answer, thanks to a revelation from God the Father. The word *Christ* means: "anointed one." In fulfillment of the Old Testament prophecies, Jesus is anointed priest (Exodus 29:7), prophet (1 Samuel 16:13), and king (1 Samuel 16:19). Jesus is the Christ of God—Priest, Prophet, and King.

Jesus foretells His suffering. *The Son of man must suffer many things, and be rejected by the elders and chief priests and scribes, and be killed, and on the third day be raised* (Luke 9:22). Rather than the political or conquering hero they expect, Jesus will be the "suffering servant" (Isaiah 52:13ff). After indicating the suffering that He will willingly embrace, Jesus gives an explanation of discipleship and an invitation to <u>everyone.</u> *And he said to <u>all</u>, "If any man would come after me, let him deny himself and take up his cross daily and follow me"* (Luke 9:23).

This message could not be more counter-cultural in modern society. Western culture promotes enhancing self-esteem as a means to find happiness. Every child is special, as evidenced by the "My child is an honor student" bumper stickers. Each child is encouraged to do what he feels is right, to express himself. In any school, listen to the number of times you will hear, "Mine." Sadly, this self-absorbed society suffers high rates of sexually transmitted diseases, depression, and suicide. Amish culture, on the other hand, encourages virtue, hard work, and service toward others, resulting in happy, well-behaved children, and low incidence of disease.

For whoever would save his life will lose it; and whoever loses his life for my sake, he will save it (Luke 9:24). The paradox Jesus reveals suggests that self-interest seldom brings true happiness. Self-concern tends to blind people to their divine purpose and ultimate destiny. Self-denial, service to others, and putting others' needs first demonstrates Christ-like behavior and brings true joy. People serving in soup kitchens often smile and laugh more than people roaming around alone in a shopping mall. Many self-help books offer the antithesis of Jesus' invitation to discipleship. Self-help books sell well, but often do not bring real contentment. Jesus provides a prescription for genuine joy: (1) deny yourself, (2) take up your cross daily, and (3) follow Jesus.

Only with the help of God's grace can anyone faithfully live as a disciple of Jesus. It may sometimes be difficult to live as a Catholic, but it is glorious to die as one. True discipleship requires God's grace and assistance.

Later, when the disciples argue about who will be the greatest, Jesus takes a child, and says, *Whoever receives this child in my name receives me, and whoever receives me receives him who sent me; for he who is least among you all is the one who is great* (Luke 9:48). Children have no power or status. They do not govern nations. Children may be seen as burdens or inconveniences. But children are lovable. Adults like to hug a child, and children love to be kissed and held. Jesus, the model of humility and self-sacrifice, turns the world's wisdom upside down. To accept and care for a child is to accept Jesus and stand affirmed before God the Father. To be a Christian, one must accept God's love as a child receives the love of his parents, and share that love with others.

The Transfiguration (Luke 9:28–36)—Peter, James, and John are privileged with a direct encounter with the divine. Luke links Jesus praying on the mountain with His transcendent transformation into dazzling glory. Some have theological knowledge of the Gospel, without an actual experience of the love that flows from a personal bond with Jesus. Knowledge, without experiencing a true relationship with Jesus, does not transform. Peter, James, and John accompany, eat, sleep, and travel with Jesus. Now, Jesus draws them deeper into the mystery of God. Their intimacy with Jesus and experience of His love transforms them. Human minds cannot fully comprehend the divine. Prayer, silence, and meditation draw the heart and the mind into communion with God. The Transfiguration strengthens the Apostles for the difficulties and crises to come.

Moses and Elijah, the law and the prophets, appeared with the Lord in conversation with him. This was in order to fulfill exactly, through the presence of these five men, the text, which says: *Before two or three witnesses every word is ratified.* . . . The radiance of the transfiguration reveals clearly and unmistakably the one, who had been promised by signs foretelling him under the veils of mystery. As Saint John says: *The law was given through Moses, grace and truth came through Jesus Christ.* In him the promise made through the shadows of prophecy stands revealed, along with the full meaning of the precepts of the law. He is the one who teaches the truth of prophecy through his presence, and makes obedience to the commandments possible through grace. . . .

He was also providing a firm foundation for the hope of holy Church. The whole body of Christ was to understand the kind of transformation that it would receive as his gift. The members of that body were to look forward to a share in that glory which first blazed out in Christ their head. The Lord had himself spoken of this when he foretold the splendor of his coming: *Then the just will shine like the sun in the kingdom of their Father.*

Pope Saint Leo the Great, *Sermon*, 51. 8, 3, 4

Jesus' countenance changes, and He appears radiant and dazzling. Moses, who received the Law, and Elijah, the father of the prophets, appear with Jesus on the mountaintop. In the Old Testament, after Moses received the Ten Commandments and came down from Mount Sinai, his face shone because he had been talking with God (Exodus 34:29). Similarly, Christians who spend time with God in prayer should become transformed and radiate the glory of God. *And we all, with unveiled face, beholding the glory of the Lord, are being changed into his likeness from one degree of glory to another; for this comes from the Lord who is the Spirit* (2 Corinthians 3:18). You have probably seen Christians who radiate the glory of God. Many people desire to be Christ-like, to be transformed into His likeness, to be radiant. But, how many people are willing to invest the time and effort to sit at His feet, to gaze upon His countenance, and to listen to Him?

After experiencing the Transfiguration, the Apostles fall silent. Profound religious experiences can best be absorbed in quiet reflection. Similarly, it can be difficult to put into words a deep spiritual encounter. Beholding Jesus in glory prefigures the glory that Christ wishes to share. Christians believe in the resurrection of the body, and wonder what they will be like in the next world. *But our commonwealth is in heaven, and from it we await a Savior, the Lord Jesus Christ, who will change our lowly body to be like his glorious body, by the power which enables him even to subject all things to himself* (Philippians 3:20–21). *Then the righteous will shine like the sun in the kingdom of their Father* (Matthew 13:43). One day we may shine with Him.

Glory is the fruit of grace: the grace possessed by Jesus in an infinite degree is reflected in an infinite glory transfiguring Him entirely. Something similar happens to us: grace will transform us "from glory to glory" (2 Corinthians 3:18), until one day it will bring us to the Beatific Vision of God in heaven. But while grace transfigures us, sin, on the other hand, darkens and disfigures whoever becomes its victim. . . .

Spiritual consolations are never an end in themselves, and we should neither desire them nor try to retain them for our own satisfaction. Joy, even that which is spiritual, should never be sought for itself. Just as in heaven, joy will be the necessary concomitant of possessing God, so too on earth, it should be nothing but a means, enabling us to give ourselves with greater generosity to the service of God. . . . God does not console us for our entertainment, but rather for our encouragement, for our strengthening, for the increase of our generosity in suffering for love of Him.

Father Gabriel of Saint Mary Magdalen, OCD, *Divine Intimacy*
(London: Baronius Press, 2008), 298–299

After the Transfiguration, a man in the crowd approaches Jesus with a humble request. *Teacher, I beg you to look upon my son, for he is my only child; and behold, a spirit seizes him, and he suddenly cries out, it convulses him till he foams, and shatters him, and will hardly leave him. And I begged your disciples to cast it out, but they could not* (Luke 9:38–40). Just as the widow of Nain lost her only child (Luke 7:12), and Jairus' only child was dying (Luke 8:42), this man seeks deliverance for his only son. Mark suggests that this kind of spirit can only be driven out by prayer and fasting (Mark 9:29). Perhaps Jesus' frustration with the disciples is due to the fact that they have not prayed to God adequately, before trying to minister to the boy and deliver him from the demon. Ministry must be constantly grounded in prayer and covered in prayer to access God's power.

The boy's father demonstrates heroic virtue. He loves his son. He asks the disciples to pray for him. When his son remains tormented, he goes directly to Jesus and asks Him for help. How often do people pray, but fail to persevere? If an immediate healing, or a spontaneous solution to a problem cannot be seen, do not give up. Rather, continue to humbly ask, to seek Jesus, to fast, and to pray. Be steadfast and tenacious as this father was persistent in seeking and asking.

The journey to Jerusalem begins—*When the days drew near for him to be received up, he set his face to go to Jerusalem* (Luke 9:51). This verse indicates a turning point in the Gospel. The first part of Luke's Gospel recounted Jesus' early life and miracles. At this point, Jesus begins His journey toward Jerusalem and the Cross. Now, Luke will focus on the teachings of Jesus. Do not try to reconstruct the exact itinerary of the journey, because this expedition is literal, geographical, and spiritual. The ultimate destination for Jesus is heaven after the Cross. Jesus fully understands this destiny. He has spoken clearly about impending suffering and death. Back at the Transfiguration, Moses and Elijah *appeared in glory and spoke of his exodus, which he was to accomplish at Jerusalem* (Luke 9:31). Jesus knew by what means He would depart from this world and return to the Father. He knew He would suffer.

Just as Jesus encountered opposition earlier in the Galilean ministry (Luke 4:16–30), now He meets with opposition in the early stages of His journey to Jerusalem. The most direct route from Galilee to Jerusalem is through Samaria. Because Jews and Samaritans do not get along, this route is dangerous for Jews. But Jesus sends messengers ahead, who learn that the Samaritans will not receive Him and allow them to pass through. James and John, the sons of thunder want Jesus to call down fire from heaven to consume them. Elijah had twice called down fire from heaven to destroy his enemies (2 Kings 1:10, 12), a captain and fifty men. The disciples want to replay this scenario, but Jesus will have none of it. He rebukes them.

On the way, Jesus meets two potential disciples. One volunteers to follow Jesus, but he hesitates. The second is called by Jesus and invited to follow, but this man has conditions. Discipleship requires forsaking everything to follow Jesus. Conditions and bargaining with God present obstacles to abandonment to God. Just as the Son of man was born in obscurity, without shelter, now as an adult Jesus remains a homeless wanderer, an itinerant preacher, with His heart set on the next world.

The Transfiguration

All three Synoptic Gospels create a link between Peter's confession and the account of Jesus' Transfiguration. . . . Let us turn now to the text of the Transfiguration narrative itself. There we are told that Jesus took Peter, James, and John and led them up onto a high mountain by themselves (Mark 9:2). We will come across these three again on the Mount of Olives (Mark 14:33) during Jesus' agony in the garden, which is the counter-image of the Transfiguration, although the two scenes are inextricably linked. . . .

Once again the mountain serves—as it did in the Sermon on the Mount and in the nights spent by Jesus in prayer—as the locus of God's particular closeness. Once again we need to keep together in our minds the various mountains of Jesus' life: the mountain of the temptation; the mountain of the Transfiguration; the mountain of his agony; the mountain of the Cross; and finally the mountain of the Risen Lord, where he declares—in total antithesis to the offer of world dominion through the devil's power: "All power in heaven and on earth is given to me" (Matthew 28:18). . . .

The mountain is the place of ascent—not only outward, but also inward ascent; it is a liberation from the burden of everyday life, a breathing in of the pure air of creation; it offers a view of the broad expanse of creation and its beauty; it gives one an inner peak to stand on and an intuitive sense of the Creator. History then adds to all this the experience of the God who speaks, and the experience of the Passion, culminating in the sacrifice of Isaac, in the sacrifice of the lamb that points ahead to the definitive Lamb sacrificed on Mount Calvary. Moses and Elijah were privileged to receive God's Revelation on the mountain, and now they are conversing with the One who is God's Revelation in person. . . .

The Transfiguration is a prayer event; it displays visibly what happens when Jesus talks with his Father: the profound interpenetration of his being with God, which then becomes pure light. . . .

"We preach Christ crucified, a stumbling block to Jews and folly to Gentiles, but to those who are called, both Jews and Greeks, Christ the power *[dynamis]* of God and the wisdom of God" (1 Corinthians 1:23ff). This "power" of the coming of the Kingdom appears to them in the transfigured Jesus, who speaks with the witnesses of the Old Covenant about the necessity of his Passion as the way to glory (Luke 24:26ff). They personally experience the anticipation of the Parousia, and that is how they are slowly initiated into the full depth of the mystery of Jesus.

Pope Benedict XVI, *Jesus of Nazareth*
(New York: Doubleday, 2007), 305–318.

1. What can you learn about the Twelve?

Luke 9:1–6
CCC 551

2. Describe Herod's perplexity. Luke 9:7–9

3. What happened in Bethsaida? Luke 9:10–17

4. Identify the verbs in the following passages.

Luke 9:16
Luke 22:19
Luke 24:30

5. What is the significance of Peter's declaration?

Luke 9:18–20
CCC 552
CCC 2600

6. What does Jesus foretell in Luke 9:22?

7. What does conversion require?

Luke 9:23–24
CCC 1435

8. Describe the coming of the Son of man in glory.

Luke 9:26
1 Thessalonians 4:16–18

9. Explain the sequence of events in Luke 9:28–36.

Luke 9:28–29
Luke 9:30–31
Luke 9:32–33
Luke 9:34–35
Luke 9:36

10. How does Peter recall this event? 2 Peter 1:16–18

11. Explain some theological aspects of the Transfiguration.

CCC 554	
CCC 555	
CCC 556	

12. What virtue does the father of the boy with a demon have?

Luke 9:37–42	
CCC 161, 162	
CCC 2728, 2742	

13. What resulted from the father's perseverance? Luke 9:42–43

* What helps you to persevere in prayer?

14. What does Jesus again foretell in Luke 9:44–45?

15. Find a contemporary application of Jesus' words in Luke 9:48a.

16. Explain Jesus' words in Luke 9:50.

17. What Old Testament event did James and John want to re-enact?

2 Kings 1:9–16
Luke 9:51–56

18. What invitation does Jesus give in Luke 9:59?

19. Define "disciple."

*What can you do to become a better disciple of Jesus?

20. What does discipleship involve?

Luke 9:60–62
CCC 520
CCC 562

CHAPTER 10

Mission
Luke 10

Whenever you enter a town and they receive you, eat what is set before you;
heal the sick in it and say to them,
"The kingdom of God has come near to you."
Luke 10:8–9

The mission of the seventy—After Jesus sends out the twelve Apostles to *preach the kingdom of God and to heal* (Luke 9:2), He then sends seventy emissaries out to proclaim the Gospel. Who are these seventy? Most of these missionaries remain unnamed in the Bible. Later, however, Luke reports Cleopas and his companion on the road to Emmaus, sharing their hopes that Jesus would be the Messiah, and women of their company said that He lives. When Peter suggested the Apostles complete their complement of twelve, and choose someone who had accompanied Jesus from the time of His baptism, *they put forward two, Joseph called Barsabbas, who was surnamed Justus, and Matthias* (Acts 1:23). So perhaps Cleopas, Joseph, and Matthias were among the seventy. These men preached the Gospel and healed people everywhere they went.

Jesus sends them out *two by two* to provide mutual support and encouragement, to witness to the truth of the Gospel with their testimony, and to become a living example of the Gospel of peace. Christians often think of missionaries as those religious who are sent to foreign lands. Saint John Paul II promised a new springtime of evangelization. Are you a missionary, or are you private about your faith, while Christians around the world are dying for their faith? If you were accused of being a Christian, would there be enough evidence to convict you? Are you reluctant or eager to share your faith with others? Do you know what to say? Pope Francis calls every baptized person to become a missionary.

> In virtue of their baptism, all the members of the People of God have become missionary disciples. . . . The new evangelization calls for personal involvement on the part of each of the baptized. Every Christian is challenged, here and now, to be actively engaged in evangelization; indeed, anyone who has truly experienced God's saving love does not need much . . . training to go out and proclaim that love.
> Pope Francis, Apostolic Exhortation on The Joy of the Gospel
> *Evangelii Gaudium* (November 24, 2013), 120

What is the message? Jesus said, *I must preach the good news of the kingdom of God* (Luke 4:43). Mark makes the message very concise: *The time is fulfilled, and the kingdom of God is at hand; repent, and believe in the gospel* (Mark 1:15). Later, Luke recounts

Peter boldly proclaiming the Gospel: *Repent, and be baptized every one of you in the name of Jesus Christ for the forgiveness of your sins; and you shall receive the gift of the Holy Spirit* (Acts 2:38). Saint Paul says, *for what we preach is not ourselves, but Jesus Christ as Lord* (2 Corinthians 4:5).

What is the evidence of faith in Jesus? Joy. *The seventy returned with joy* (Luke 10:17). Why should you share the good news? Saint John Paul II said, "Faith is strengthened when it is given to others" (*Redemptoris Missio,* December 7, 1990, 2). Do you want more joy? Do you want your faith strengthened? Learn how to share your faith. Pray to the Holy Spirit for courage and opportunities to evangelize. And while you are sharing your faith with someone who is on God's heart, He might send someone to share the faith with someone who is on your heart.

The Gospel Message

God loves you. *For God so loved the world that he gave his only-begotten Son, that whoever believes in him should not perish but have eternal life* (John 3:16).

Sin breaks our relationship with God. *All have sinned and fall short of the glory of God* (Romans 3:23).

Jesus paid the price for all sin. *Christ also died for sins once for all, the righteous for the unrighteous, that he might bring us to God, being put to death in the flesh but made alive in the spirit* (1 Peter 3:18).

Repent and Jesus will restore you. *If we confess our sins, he is faithful and just, and will forgive our sins and cleanse us from all unrighteousness* (1 John 1:9).

Learn ways to share the Gospel in just a few minutes. Memorizing just a few Scripture passages will help. Develop a relationship with someone. Become interested in the life and concerns of another. Share a meal or a cup of coffee. Offer a smile, some small service, help in a time of need. Love and joy evidence the presence of God. People might ask you the source of your strength and joy, and then you will be prepared to share your faith and proclaim the Gospel.

He who hears you hears me, and he who rejects you rejects me, and he who rejects me rejects him who sent me (Luke 10:16). These sobering words underscore the importance of loyal submission to the magisterium of the Church—the Holy Father, the successor of Peter, and the bishops, successors of the Apostles in union with him. The will of God comes to us in the commandments, and through the pope and bishops who speak in God's Name. "One of the greatest obstacles to full conformity of our will to God's is our attachment to our own desires and inclinations. Obedience makes us this happy exchange: renunciation of our will for God's will." (Father Gabriel, OCD, *Divine Intimacy*, 343).

When the seventy return from their successful missionary activity with joy, Jesus tells them to *rejoice that your names are written in heaven* (Luke 10:20). Jesus rejoices and thanks the Father. Luke 10:21 recounts the only place in the Bible in which Jesus rejoices. The faithful proclamation of the Gospel and the conversion of sinners bring great joy to Jesus.

The Parable of the Good Samaritan—Even non-Christians, who may have never opened a Bible, use the language "Good Samaritan" to refer to someone who helps a stranger in distress. Pope Emeritus Benedict XVI offers beautiful commentary on this very familiar parable.

The Good Samaritan

The story of the Good Samaritan concerns the fundamental human question. A lawyer—a master of exegesis—poses this question to the Lord: *Teacher, what shall I do to inherit eternal life?* (Luke 10:25). Luke comments that the scholar addresses this question to Jesus in order to put him to the test. Being a Scripture scholar himself, he knows how the Bible answers his question, but he wants to see what this prophet without formal biblical studies has to say about it. The Lord very simply refers him to the Scripture, which of course he knows, and gets him to give the answer himself. The scholar does so by combining Deuteronomy 6:5 and Leviticus 19:18, and he is right on target: *You shall love the Lord your God with all your heart . . . and your neighbor as yourself* (Luke 10:27). . . .

But now the learned man, who knew the answer to his own question perfectly well, has to justify himself. What the Scripture says is uncontroversial, but how it is to be applied in practice in daily life raises questions. . . . The concrete question is who is meant by "neighbor". . . .

The road from Jerusalem to Jericho turns out to be an image of human history; the half-dead man lying by the side of it is an image of humanity. . . . If the assault victim is the image of Everyman, the Samaritan can only be the image of Jesus Christ. God himself, who for us is foreign and distant, has set out to take care of his wounded creature. God, though remote from us, has made himself our neighbor in Jesus Christ. He pours oil and wine into our wound, a gesture seen as an image of the healing gift of the sacraments, and he brings us into the inn, the Church. . . .

We realize that we are all "alienated," in need of redemption. Now we realize that we are all in need of the gift of God's redeeming love ourselves, so that we too can become "lovers" in our turn. . . . Everyone must first be healed and filled with God's gifts. But then everyone is also called to become a Samaritan—to follow Christ and become like him. When we do that, we live rightly. We love rightly when we become like him, who loved all of us first.

Pope Benedict XVI, *Jesus of Nazareth* (NY: Doubleday, 2007), 194–201

Martha and Mary, and their brother Lazarus, were friends of Jesus, living in the town of Bethany, about two miles east of Jerusalem. The familiar story of Martha and Mary is probably not a favorite of many hard-working women. Mary sat at the Lord's feet and listened to His teaching, while Martha was busy and distracted with much serving. She was probably cleaning, preparing food, cooking, setting the table, washing the pots, and serving the food. Martha complains and asks Jesus to get Mary to help her with the work. Jesus' answer is also familiar, *Martha, Martha, you are anxious and troubled about many things; one thing is needful. Mary has chosen the good portion, which shall not be taken away from her* (Luke 10:41).

The Church has often seen Martha and Mary as representatives of the active life and the contemplative life, respectively. Most Christians must strive to balance these two dimensions. A life of prayer that ignores the needs of others, or an active life of service that neglects prayer, becomes imbalanced. Jesus gives the perfect example of deep prayer preceding compassionate and fruitful ministry. Throughout the Christian life, believers reflect and discern whether prayer and service are in proper balance, or whether adjustments should be made.

Martha is redeemed in John's Gospel: *Now Jesus loved Martha and her sister and Lazarus* (John 11:5). Jesus loves Martha. He mentions Martha first. After the death of Lazarus, it is Martha who runs to Jesus while Mary stays home. Then, Martha makes a profession of faith, as clear and bold as Peter's. *Yes, Lord; I believe that you are the Christ, the Son of God, he who is coming into the world* (John 11:27). Apparently, Martha has taken the Lord's correction to heart.

In modern times, some people have suggested that Jesus was restricted by the cultural mores and norms of His time, which constrained His ministry to women. Nothing could be further from the truth, and this pericope disproves that theory. In Bethany, Jesus behaves contrary to Jewish cultural norms. Jesus is alone with two women in their home, Martha and Mary, who are not relatives. Lazarus may be at work or away, but he is not mentioned as being present. Jesus teaches a woman in her home and allows her to sit at His feet. Jesus also ministers to a sinful Samaritan woman alone at Jacob's well (John 4:4ff). No rabbi would do those things!

Jesus is not a misogynist. Luke's Gospel provides many examples of Jesus talking with women, healing women, teaching women, and visiting with women. As Martha serves Jesus, the theme of Jesus enjoying table fellowship emerges. Luke develops this favorite theme of Jesus dining in at least seven places in his Gospel (Luke 5:29–39; 7:36–50; 11:37–54; 14:1–24; 19:1–10; 22:14–20; 24:13–35). Often when Jesus arrives as a dinner guest, the tables are turned and the guest becomes the dominant figure, who answers questions, gives teachings and lessons, and even works miracles at the table.

Mary of Bethany has chosen the better part. She sits at the Lord's feet listening to Him teach. Mary illustrates a contemplative dimension of prayer. She sits silently in the Lord's presence to listen. For many Christians, prayer becomes a one-way monologue.

People say their prayers. But prayer involves talking to and also *listening to God*. Setting aside time to sit silently and listen to the Lord, especially in the presence of the Blessed Sacrament, can make a perfect application of this Scripture to one's personal life.

Good Samaritan Charity

How can we fail to mention all those daily gestures of openness, sacrifice and unselfish care which countless people lovingly make in families, hospitals, orphanages, homes for the elderly and other centers or communities which defend life? Allowing herself to be guided by the example of Jesus the "Good Samaritan" (cf. Luke 10:29–37) and upheld by his strength, the Church has always been in the front line in providing charitable help: so many of her sons and daughters . . . freely giving of themselves out of love for their neighbor, especially for the weak and needy. These deeds strengthen the bases of the "civilization of love and life," without which the life of individuals and of society itself loses its most genuinely human quality. Even if they go unnoticed and remain hidden to most people, faith assures us that the Father "who sees in secret" (Matthew 6:6) not only will reward these actions but already here and now makes them produce lasting fruit for the good of all. . . .

In our service of charity, we must be inspired and distinguished by a specific attitude: we must care for the other as a person for whom God has made us responsible. As disciples of Jesus, we are called to become neighbors to everyone (cf. Luke 10:29–37), and to show special favor to those who are poorest, most alone and most in need. In helping the hungry, the thirsty, the foreigner, the naked, the sick, the imprisoned—as well as the child in the womb and the old person who is suffering or near death—we have the opportunity to serve Jesus.

He himself said: "As you did it to one of the least of these my brethren, you did it to me" (Matthew 25:40). Hence we cannot but feel called to account and judge by the ever relevant words of Saint John Chrysostom: "Do you wish to honor the body of Christ? Do not neglect it when you find it naked. Do not do it homage here in the church with silk fabrics only to neglect it outside where it suffers cold and nakedness."

Saint John Paul II, The Gospel of Life *Evangelium Vitae*
(March 25, 1995), 27.2, 87.2

1. What did Jesus set in motion? How is the kingdom advanced?

Luke 10:1–9
CCC 765
CCC 2611

2. Explain Luke 10:2–3 in your own words. Give examples.

3. Compare the following verses.

1 Samuel 25:6
Luke 10:5

4. Apply the passage below to contemporary life.

Luke 10:7
CCC 2122

5. Explain the mission of the disciples. Luke 10:9

6. What can you learn from the following verses?

Luke 10:16
CCC 87–88
CCC 858

7. With what emotion did the disciples return? Where can you get this?

Luke 10:17
CCC 30
CCC 736

8. Find a common image in these passages.

Luke 10:18
Revelation 12:9

9. Why should you rejoice? Luke 10:20

* What is the difference between joy and happiness? How can you get more joy?

10. What did Jesus do in Luke 10:21a?

* How does one rejoice in the Holy Spirit? CCC 733

11. What can you learn from these verses?

Luke 10:21b
1 Corinthians 1:26–29
James 2:5

12. What did Jesus tell the disciples privately? What does this mean?

Luke 10:23–24
1 Peter 1:10–12

** Jesus gives His disciples a mission. What is your mission?

13. What did the lawyer call Jesus and why did he approach Jesus? Luke 10:25

14. What must one do to inherit eternal life? Luke 10:27

Deuteronomy 6:5	
Leviticus 19:18b	
Romans 13:8	
Galatians 5:14–15	
James 2:8–9	

15. Outline the parable of the Good Samaritan.

Luke 10:30	
Luke 10:31–32	
Luke 10:33–35	
Luke 10:36	
Luke 10:37	

* Why do you think the lawyer asked Jesus, "Who is my neighbor?"

16. What is unusual about Luke 10:38–39 in Jesus' time?

17. What can you learn about Martha?

Luke 10:38–40
John 11:5
John 11:20
John 11:21–27
John 12:1–3

18. What can you learn about Mary?

Luke 10:39, 42
John 11:20b
John 12:3

19. What did Jesus say? Luke 10:41–42

20. Mary represents prayer, and Martha represents service. How much time do you spend in prayer? How much time in serving others? Do you need more balance?

CHAPTER 11

Prayer
Luke 11

When you pray, say:
"Father, hallowed be your name.
Your kingdom come.
Give us each day our daily bread;
and forgive us our sins,
for we ourselves forgive every one who is indebted to us;
and lead us not into temptation."
Luke 11:2–4

The Lord's Prayer—Jesus was praying, and one of the disciples asked for instruction in prayer. Prayer is a dominant theme in Luke's Gospel. Luke shows Jesus regularly drawing apart for private prayer before every major event of His ministry. Prayer demonstrates an inborn desire for unity with God, consistent with the search for meaning and happiness. The Lord's Prayer in Matthew follows the Sermon on the Mount and is longer, five verses compared to two verses in Luke.

The Lord's Prayer	

Our Father who art in heaven.
Hallowed be thy name.
Thy kingdom come.
Thy will be done,
  On earth as it is in heaven.
Give us this day our daily bread;
And forgive us our trespasses,
  As we forgive those
    who trespass against us;
And lead us not into temptation,
  But deliver us from evil.
 	
(Matthew 6:9–13)
	Father, hallowed be your name.
	Your kingdom come.
	Give us each day our daily bread;
	  and forgive us our sins,
	for we ourselves
	  forgive every one
	  who is indebted to us;
	and lead us not into temptation.
	
	(Luke 11:2–4)

It is not surprising that Jesus would give a similar teaching on prayer at different times. You may have also heard variant forms of the same prayer at different times. For example, the Prayer to Saint Michael the Archangel asks him to be a "protector" or "safeguard." By the power of God, he will "cast" or "thrust" into hell Satan and all the evil spirits, who "prowl" or "roam" about the world.

Jesus invites disciples to call His Father, "Our Father." Thanks to Jesus, we become a family of believers. Jesus does not invite one to pray "My Father," as if Christianity was a solitary enterprise, but to pray in union with the Church. *Hallowed be your name* reflects the first commandment, to love and honor God above all and to desire God's kingdom more than personal desires. *Give us each day our daily bread* refers to material sustenance, food for the body, as well as spiritual food to sustain the soul—the Word of God and the Blessed Sacrament. Christians share the mercy and forgiveness that God has first given. *"Lead us not into temptation"* does not suggest that God tempts, *for God cannot be tempted with evil and he himself tempts no one* (James 1:13). Temptations come to all people. Resisting temptation tests our fidelity to God and develops growth in virtue.

> The words of the Our Father give a concrete model, which is also a universal model. In fact, everything that can and must be said to the Father is contained in those seven requests, which we all know by heart. There is such a simplicity in them that even a child can learn them, but at the same time such a depth that a whole life can be spent meditating on their meaning. Isn't that so? Does not each of those petitions deal with something essential to our life, directing it totally towards God the Father? Doesn't this prayer speak to us about "our daily bread," "forgiveness of our sins, since we forgive others," and about protecting us from "temptations" and "delivering us from evil?"
>
> Saint John Paul II, *General Audience,* March 14, 1979

Luke follows with an exhortation to persevere in prayer. The parables of the friend at midnight (Luke 11:5–8) and the unjust judge (Luke 18:1–8) demonstrate the importance of persevering in prayer. The heavenly Father will give the Holy Spirit, the best gift that the believer can receive, to those who persevere (Luke 11:13).

> When the Lord is present, all goes well and nothing seems hard to do for His love; but when He is absent, everything is difficult. When Jesus does not speak to our soul, no other consolation suffices; but if He speaks only one word, we feel inner joy. . . . It is a great art to know how to talk with Jesus, and to know how to keep Him with you is great wisdom. Be humble and peaceful and Jesus will be with you; be devout and quiet and He will stay with you. . . .
>
> Of all who are dear to you, let Jesus be your best beloved. All others must be loved for Jesus' sake, but Jesus for Himself alone. Jesus Christ must be loved exclusively, for He alone is proved good and faithful above all other friends.
>
> Thomas à Kempis, *The Imitation of Christ* (New York: Catholic Book, 1977), 80

God is the source of genuine lasting happiness. Prayer increases one's capacity to experience God's love. This entails hard work. Prayer raises one's thoughts and mind to God, and asks good things of God. Saint Thérèse, the Little Flower, said, "For me, prayer is a surge of the heart; it is a simple look turned toward heaven, it is a cry of recognition and of love, embracing both trial and joy" (CCC 2558). Prayer involves talking to *and listening to* God. Jesus gives more than a formula for prayer. He demonstrates an attitude for prayer and reveals His relationship in prayer. Along with vocal prayer, Jesus spent time in silent prayer and meditation. A perfect way to grow in the spiritual life is to make a personal prayer time every day, setting aside time to listen to God in silence.

Kingdoms in conflict—No one doubts that Jesus has cast a demon out of a mute man (Luke 11:14), but they challenge the source of Jesus' power. They accuse Jesus of casting out demons by the power of Be-el′zebul, the prince of demons. Jesus points out their faulty logic. Why would Satan work against himself and destroy his own evil? *But if it is by the finger of God that I cast out demons, then the kingdom of God has come upon you* (Luke 11:20). When Moses and Aaron introduced the plagues in Egypt, *the magicians said to Pharaoh, "This is the finger of God"* (Exodus 8:19). Jesus explains that even though Satan is like a strong man, He can overpower the devil. Believers have nothing to fear. The kingdom of God is at hand. Jesus is greater and stronger than any other force on earth, even the forces of evil.

Paul assures us that we are more than conquerors in Jesus. *For I am sure that neither death, nor life, nor angels, nor principalities, nor things present, nor things to come, nor powers, nor height, nor depth, nor anything else in all creation, will be able to separate us from the love of God in Christ Jesus our Lord* (Romans 8:38–39). James gives practical advice against evil: *Resist the devil and he will flee from you. Draw near to God and he will draw near to you* (James 4:7b–8). Peter cautions believers to be diligent and alert against evil: *Be sober, be watchful. Your adversary the devil prowls around like a roaring lion, seeking some one to devour. Resist him, firm in your faith, knowing that the same experience of suffering is required of your brotherhood throughout the world* (1 Peter 5:8–9). Don't be caught off guard!

Drawing near to God and obtaining grace fills the spiritual void created by the unclean spirit. After being exorcised, the person must choose to call on God so that his soul will be filled with grace, and the evil spirit cannot return. Never trifle or dabble with evil. Failure to eliminate evil, dabbling with the occult, leaving a door open even a crack for darkness, can leave a person in serious danger, worse than before (Luke 11:24–26).

The sign of Jonah—People demand a sign from Jesus (Luke 11:16). They test Him and want to see a sign from heaven. But Jesus will not be manipulated. They will only be given the sign of Jonah. When Jonah proclaimed God's Word to the people of Nineveh, they believed and repented. Everyone, from the king on the throne to the common people, fasted and prayed to God for mercy. Jesus is greater than Jonah. The people see miracles, yet they refuse to repent and believe in Jesus. Therefore, judgment and condemnation await them.

People refuse to see what is right in front of their eyes. *Your eye is the lamp of your body; when your eye is sound, your whole body is full of light; but when it is not sound, your body is full of darkness* (Luke 11:34). People see what they want to see, and ignore what they choose to ignore. Even today, people call what is good evil, and what is evil good. Tolerance has become the supreme virtue, where righteousness and the things of God are the only intolerable things that remain.

Jesus denounces the hypocrisy of the Pharisees and lawyers—The Pharisees knew the Scriptures. They could see Jesus fulfilling the prophecies: giving sight to the blind, enabling the lame to walk, and the deaf to hear. They could have helped the common people understand the fulfillment of the prophecies, but they blocked the way of those who wanted to believe and follow Jesus. They were so focused on the small things they thought were wrong that they missed the great miracle.

The Pharisee was astonished to see that he did not first wash before dinner (Luke 11:38). One should not assume that Jesus came to the table with dirty hands, any more than a priest comes to celebrate Mass unwashed. The Pharisees' hand washing was a symbolic ritual, not the actual removal of dirt, as a surgeon scrubs before surgery. Jesus makes a point in rejecting their ritual washings, while pointing out their inner dispositions. *But give alms for those things which are within; and behold, everything is clean for you* (Luke 11:41). Giving alms pleases God. The Archangel Raphael told Tobit: *Prayer is good when accompanied by fasting, almsgiving, and righteousness. . . . Almsgiving delivers from death, and it will purge away every sin* (Tobit 12:8, 9). *Water extinguishes a blazing fire: so almsgiving atones for sin* (Sirach 3:30).

Jesus accuses the Pharisees of tithing spices—like rue, a small, bitter medicinal plant—but neglecting the greater matters concerning love of God and justice. Prestige gained from the best seat in the synagogue does not reflect authentic virtue or interior conversion. Jesus speaks just as harshly to the lawyers, who impose burdensome regulations on the people, rather than seeking genuine justice and piety. The blood of Abel (Luke 11:51) results from the first crime of fratricide, when Cain killed his brother (Genesis 4:8). Zechariah the prophet was stoned in the temple around 800 BC when he confronted the people with their sins against God (2 Chronicles 24:20–21). The blood of Abel and Zechariah represent the earliest and latest murders in the Hebrew Scriptures.

Woe to you lawyers! for you have taken away the key of knowledge; you did not enter yourselves, and you hindered those who were entering (Luke 11:52). These doctors of the Law could read the prophecies concerning the Messiah. Most of the common people could not read. These lawyers and Pharisees should have assisted the people in comparing the prophecies of the Messiah with the life of Jesus. They could have helped the people, but they hindered them instead.

Hypocrisy is a form of lying in which a person pretends to have virtues or moral character that he does not possess. Duplicity offends God. Humility and a frequent, honest examination of conscience helps believers avoid the trap of insincerity. Sincere love of

God and neighbor require honesty. Almsgiving pleases God. Jesus shows kindness in pointing out their sin from which they could have repented. *Whoever brings back a sinner from the error of his way will save his soul from death and will cover a multitude of sins* (James 5:20). Following Jesus' example, speak the truth in love (Ephesians 4:15) to those living in obvious, serious sin. *Above all hold unfailing your love for one another, since love covers a multitude of sins* (1 Peter 4:8). Love lavishly, shun hypocrisy, and give alms generously.

The Prayer of Jesus

Although Jesus was always indissolubly united to His Father by the Beatific Vision and the plentitude of charity, He willed to consecrate to Him exclusively a part of His human activity: the time of prayer. The long years spent at Nazareth and the forty days in the desert were especially consecrated to prayer, and during His apostolic life Jesus usually prayed during the whole or part of the night. The Gospel clearly notes this prayer of Christ at the more solemn moments of His life: before He chose the twelve Apostles, Jesus "went out into a mountain to pray, and He passed the whole night in the prayer of God" (Luke 6:12). He prayed before Peter's confession, before the Transfiguration, at the Last Supper, in Gethsemane, on Calvary. Moreover, He frequently interrupted His apostolic activity to retire into the desert to pray. . . .

We cannot imagine a more intimate and profound prayer than the prayer of Jesus. Only in heaven, where it will be given us also to see God face to face, shall we be able to understand it and really participate in it. But even here on earth we can imitate the conduct of Jesus by readily interrupting any activity, even apostolic work, in order to devote to prayer the time assigned to it, leaving everything else to focus our attention on God alone. . . .

O my God, Most Holy Trinity, grant that, at least in time of prayer, I may be aware of Your presence in my soul and may make my union with You real. . . .

O Jesus, teach me and grant me that intense prayer, which immerses the soul in God and which, by living contact with Him, inflames and strengthens it. I desire to share in Your prayer, which is the only adoration worthy of God. Therefore, dear Lord, take my poor prayer; unite it to Yours and offer it to the Blessed Trinity. Only in this way can I too become one of those "true adorers . . . *in spirit and in truth*" (John 4:23) whom the Father seeks and desires.

Father Gabriel of Saint Mary Magdalen, OCD, *Divine Intimacy*
(London: Baronius Press, 2008), 165–167

1. What can you learn about prayer from the passages below?

Luke 11:1–4
CCC 2601
CCC 2759

2. Explain some aspects of "The Lord's Prayer."

CCC 2761
CCC 2763
CCC 2765
CCC 2766

3. How can a person invoke God as "Father"?

Luke 11:2
CCC 2779
CCC 2782

* How often do you pray the Lord's Prayer? Do you ever just run through it, without thinking about the words? How often do you *really* pray it?

4. Does God lead people into temptation?

| Luke 11:4 |
| James 1:13–15 |
| CCC 2846–2848 |

5. What does the parable in Luke 11:5–12 teach about prayer?

* What are your favorite prayers and devotionals—Mass, Rosary, novenas?

6. What will the heavenly Father give to those who ask? Luke 11:13

7. What is Jesus doing in Luke 11:14?

8. To whom do the people attribute Christ's power? Luke 11:15ff

9. How does Jesus respond to unjust criticism? What is the source of His power?

Luke 11:20–23
Exodus 8:19
Exodus 31:18
CCC 700

10. Find a practical application to Luke 11:24–26.

* How could a person fill the void left by evil in the soul?

11. What two things are required for blessedness? Luke 11:28

** Did the Blessed Mother fulfill those criteria? Luke 1:38, 42

12. Describe the characters below. Luke 11:29–32

Jonah (Jonah 1:1–2)
Son of man (Luke 11:30)
Queen of the South (1 Kings 10:1–10)
Men of Nineveh (Jonah 3:4–5)
Someone greater (Philippians 2:9–11)

13. Who or what gives light to your soul?

Luke 11:33–36
Psalm 119:105
Luke 1:76–79; 2:29–32
John 8:12

* How can a person tell if he or she is following the true light?

14. Explain the drama in Luke 11:37–38.

15. What does Jesus say in Luke 11:39–41?

16. Of what does Jesus accuse the Pharisees? Luke 11:42–44

17. How do the lawyers address Jesus? Luke 11:45

18. Of what does Jesus accuse the lawyers? Luke 11:45–52

19. What were the scribes and Pharisees doing? Luke 11:53–54

20. Discuss different opportunities to enhance your prayer life. Which of these might you try to incorporate into your life?

_____ Daily prayer

_____ Mass

_____ Rosary

_____ Adoration of the Blessed Sacrament

_____ Contemplative prayer

_____ Other

CHAPTER 12

Parables
Luke 12–13

And I tell you, every one who acknowledges me before men,
the Son of man also will acknowledge before the angels of God;
but he who denies me before men
will be denied before the angels of God.
Luke 12:8–9

Parables—Jesus taught, gave warnings, and often spoke in parables. A parable is a short story based on familiar life experiences and used to teach a spiritual lesson. The parable usually ends with a trigger that demands reflection, consideration, and a response or a decision to act. Luke recounts more of Jesus' parables than the other evangelists.

Jesus warns the disciples about the hypocrisy of the Pharisees. God prefers an honest, repentant sinner over a play-actor who pretends to be holy. Believers must guard against living double lives. Going to church and doing works of charity in public while hiding sinful lives in private cannot work, because God knows and sees everything. *Whatever you have said in the dark shall be heard in the light, and what you have whispered in private rooms shall be proclaimed upon the housetops* (Luke 12:3). Christians should live transparent lives. What you see is what is real.

Here in Luke 12:4 and again in John's Gospel, Jesus refers to the disciples as friends. *You are my friends if you do what I command you* (John 15:14). *I tell you, my friends, do not fear those who kill the body, and after that have no more that they can do. But I will warn you whom to fear: fear him who, after he has killed, has the power to cast into hell* (Luke 12:4–5). People naturally fear murderers and thieves, but Jesus warns believers to fear those who kill the conscience and deaden the soul. With filial love and devotion, believers must be prepared to stand up for Jesus. Denying Christ in this life to fit in with the crowd could have disastrous consequences in the next life.

Blasphemy against the Holy Spirit—*And every one who speaks a word against the Son of man will be forgiven; but he who blasphemes against the Holy Spirit will not be forgiven* (Luke 12:10). What is this unforgivable sin? Saint Thomas Aquinas says that a sin is "unforgivable by its very nature, insofar as it excludes the elements through which the forgiveness of sin takes place" *(Summa Theologiae II,* 14.3). Faith and repentance are elements required for the forgiveness of sins. Stubborn refusal to believe, repent, and accept the mercy God offers through the power of the Holy Spirit leaves one's sins unforgiven. So, refusing to believe and refusing to repent results in darkness. The sinner, who refuses to believe that God exists and refuses to acknowledge that sinful behaviors are sin, or will not accept that God has the power to forgive, blasphemes the Holy Spirit. A person who does not want to be forgiven can reject God's mercy. God honors free will.

The gift of the Holy Spirit will be a powerful help to Christians. Those believers who suffer for their faith in God can rely on the Holy Spirit to give them grace and power. Luke illustrates the powerful way in which Peter proclaims the faith after the Holy Spirit comes on Pentecost (Acts 2:14ff). The Holy Spirit also strengthens those believers with the courage to suffer martyrdom in the name of Jesus.

The Parable of the Rich Fool—A young man asks Jesus to judge between himself and his brother over their inheritance. This situation calls to mind the Parable of the Prodigal Son, in which two brothers expect an inheritance. Jesus refuses to get involved in this dispute. Throughout the centuries it seems that even before the funeral meal has been eaten, children are fighting over their parents' possessions, whether it is a pocket watch or millions of dollars. Instead of getting involved in the dispute, Jesus moves on to teach a parable about the sin of greed or avarice.

Nothing is inherently wrong with acquiring material possessions and providing for one's needs and the needs of ones' family. However, obsessive greed hinders spiritual growth. Count the number of times that the rich man uses the words "I" and "my" in these three short verses (Luke 12:17–19). This man's narcissism prevents him from focusing on God and others. *But God said to him, "Fool! This night your soul is required of you; and the things you have prepared, whose will they be?"* (Luke 12:20–21). Pope Paul VI said that, "avarice . . . is the most obvious form of stultified moral underdevelopment" (Encyclical Letter On the Development of Peoples *Populorum Progressio,* March 26, 1967, 19). It is folly to amass material goods for one's self while neglecting one's eternal salvation and the needs of others.

Practicing the spiritual and corporal works of mercy enable believers to become rich in the things of God. It is lawful to work hard and to enjoy the fruits of one's labors. Balance requires moderation in all things and generosity toward God. Real treasure is found in the sanctuary of the heart. *For where your treasure is, there will your heart be also* (Luke 12:34). Make sure that the soul is well nurtured.

Spiritual Works of Mercy	Corporal Works of Mercy
Admonish the sinner.	Feed the hungry.
Instruct the ignorant.	Give drink to the thirsty.
Counsel the doubtful.	Clothe the naked.
Comfort the sorrowful.	Visit the imprisoned.
Bear wrongs patiently.	Shelter the homeless.
Forgive all injuries.	Visit the sick.
Pray for the living and the dead.	Bury the dead.

Jesus gives examples of wise, moral living contrasted with foolish behavior in many parables. The parables provide examples of some people performing works of mercy and others acting callously. Despite the passage of centuries, these stories continue to communicate moral truths and principles for a godly life. Mark only reports a few of Jesus' parables. Matthew recalls about fifteen parables of Jesus. Luke recounts more than twenty parables. Only the Parable of the Sower and the Parable of the Mustard Seed appear in all three Synoptic Gospels.

New Testament Parables	Matthew	Mark	Luke
Children Who Play	11:16–19		7:31, 35
The Sower	13:3–8	4:3–8	8:4–8
The Weeds among the Wheat	13:24–30		
Seed Growing in Secret		4:26–30	
Mustard Seed	13:31–32	4:30–32	13:18–19
The Leaven	13:33		13:20–21
Hidden Treasure: Pearl of Great Price	13:44–45		
Dragnet	13:47–48		
Lost Sheep	18:12–14		15:4–7
Unmerciful Servant	18:23–35		7:41–43
Laborers in Vineyard	20:1–6		
Two Sons	21:28–32	12:1–11	
Wicked Tenants	21:33–44		20:9–18
Marriage Feast	22:1–14		
Wise and Foolish Virgins	25:1–13		
Talents	25:14–30		
The Good Samaritan			10:25–37
Importunate Friend			11:5–8
Rich Fool			12:16–21
Barren Fig Tree			13:6–9
Marriage Feast			14:7–14
Great Banquet			14:15–24
Tower and War			14:28–32
Lost Coin			15:8–10
The Prodigal Son			15:11–32
Dishonest Steward			16:1–8
Rich Man and Lazarus			16:19–31
The Widow and the Judge			18:1–8
Pharisee and the Publican			18:9–14
The Pounds			19:12–27

Worry is useless, since worry can change nothing. Worry does not add to the length of one's life, and in fact, stress could shorten a life. Alert watchfulness enables one to be spiritually ready at all times. Watchfulness involves a peaceful trust and reliance on God, and persistent prayer. Saint Peter exhorts: *The end of all things is at hand; therefore keep sane and sober for your prayers. Above all hold unfailing your love for one another, since love covers a multitude of sins* (1 Peter 4:7).

Luke gives the servant parables an ecclesiological application. The early Christian community must have servants who will be faithful and watchful. Luke uses the Greek word *oikonomos* for steward (Luke 12:42; 16:1, 3, 8), designating one who provides service in the Christian community. Irony occurs when the master puts on his apron and serves the servants (Luke 12:37). Surprisingly, Jesus the Master will serve the Apostles and all of humanity (Luke 22:27).

Fire on the earth—*I came to cast fire upon the earth; and would that it were already kindled* (Luke 12:49). Fire depicts God's merciful love and protection. *The LORD went before them . . . by night in a pillar of fire to give them light* (Exodus 13:21). The Lord wants to light a fire of apostolic fervor on the earth, and equip the disciples to spread the Gospel. *My heart became hot within me. As I mused, the fire burned; then I spoke with my tongue* (Psalm 39:3).

People know how to interpret the weather and the signs of the times. The signs of the coming Messiah were clearly foretold by the prophets, recorded on scrolls in the synagogues, and proclaimed. After hearing the preaching and teaching of Jesus, and watching Him perform miracles, why could they not connect the dots and come to the obvious conclusion—that Jesus is the promised Savior of Israel?

Repent and be ready—Jesus was a Galilean. Perhaps those who perished at Pilate's hand were friends or acquaintances. An accident in Siloam claimed the lives of eighteen people on whom a tower fell. Jesus warns that *unless you repent you will all likewise perish* (Luke 13:5). Everyone will taste death at some time, either by illness, accident, or old age, sooner or later. Many are caught off-guard. But, a wise person prepares. *You also must be ready; for the Son of man is coming at an hour you do not expect* (Luke 12:40). Disciples should learn from the unexpected death of others to repent and be prepared for judgment at all times.

The barren fig tree was nurtured for three years (Luke 13:6–9). Jesus ministered among the people for three years, inviting all to repent and believe in the Gospel. While God is rich in mercy and displays great patience, He is also just. Those who stubbornly persist in their refusal to repent will ultimately be cut down.

In the synagogue, on the Sabbath, Jesus heals a woman who had been crippled for eighteen years. When she is healed and can straighten up, *she praised God* (Luke 13:13). Once again, a ruler of the synagogue shows outrage that Jesus has healed on the Sabbath. Jesus points out that people care for their animals on the Sabbath, but a woman, a daughter of Abraham bound by Satan, is far more important than an ox or a donkey, which observant Jews would feed and water on the Sabbath. The leaders criticize, but the common people rejoice. Today, people can behave like the Pharisees in criticizing weak music or a mediocre homily, instead of focusing on the amazing miracle taking place on the altar—the Eucharist.

The parable of the tiny mustard seed, which grows so large, predicts the ultimate growth of the Church. This also gives encouragement to those who do small things for the glory of God. Blessed Mother Teresa said that those who are not called to do great things are called to do small things with great love. After all, salvation came to the world because one young woman accepted one Child into her life. Small acts of kindness, obedience, and faithful ministry can have extraordinary ripple effects.

The narrow door—If you have been to a funeral lately, you might be under the impression that everyone is in already heaven. Who prays for the souls of the dead? And why offer Masses for these souls if everyone is in a better place? But Jesus says, *Strive to enter by the narrow door; for many, I tell you, will seek to enter and will not be able* (Luke 13:24). The Greek word for strive, *ag nizesthe,* suggests agonizing, or striving. Christians strive to remain in the state of grace. Christian life cannot remain stagnant. The evil one constantly tries to pull believers away from God's love and mercy. Unless Christians push forward, they will backslide.

Some Pharisees come to warn Jesus that Herod wants to kill Him. Clearly, not all of the Pharisees oppose Jesus, but some are friends and followers. Luke provides a rare positive reference to Pharisees. Despite the danger, Jesus presses on in His journey toward Jerusalem and His destiny. Jesus resolutely embraces the will and plan of the Father. Nevertheless, Jesus laments over Jerusalem. Later, when Jesus approaches the city, Luke reports that Jesus weeps over Jerusalem (Luke 19:41)

Parables

Jesus' invitation to enter his kingdom comes in the form of *parables,* a characteristic feature of his teaching (cf. *Mk 4:33–34*). Through his parables he invites people to the feast of the kingdom, but he also asks for a radical choice: to gain the kingdom, one must give everything *(cf. Mt 13:44–45; 22:1–14).* Words are not enough; deeds are required (cf. *Mt 21:28–32*). The parables are like mirrors for man: will he be hard soil or good earth for the word? (cf. *Mt 13:3–9*). What use has he made of the talents he has received? (cf. *Mt 25:14–30*). Jesus and the presence of the kingdom in this world are secretly at the heart of the parables. One must enter the kingdom, that is, become a disciple of Christ, in order to "know the secrets of the kingdom of heaven" (*Mt 13:11*). For those who stay "outside," everything remains enigmatic (*Mk 4:11*; cf. *Mt 13:10–15*).

CCC 546

---

1. Use a dictionary or the Catechism to define "parable."

2. Define the sin that Jesus' warns against in Luke 12:1–2.

3. Explain the sin of blasphemy against the Holy Spirit.

Luke 12:10
CCC 1864

4. Who helps you in what you ought to say? Luke 12:12

5. Explain the parable of the rich fool. Luke 12:13–21

* How could someone become *rich toward God?* Luke 12:21

6. Why should you not be anxious or afraid? Luke 12:22–32

* What are some ways to overcome worry and anxiety?

7. Where do you find your treasure? Luke 12:33–34

8. Why should one be watchful?

Luke 12: 35–40
Matthew 24:29–31, 43–44
2 Peter 3:10–11
Revelation 3:3

9. What is fire on the earth?

Luke 12:49–53
CCC 696

10. What does Jesus command in Luke 12:57? Have you ever been judged for this?

11. How can you apply the directive in Luke 13:3–5 to your life?

Luke 13:3–5
CCC 1422

* How often do you think you should avail yourself of the above sacrament?

12. Explain the parable of the barren fig tree, and the significance of three years.

13. Describe the conflict in the drama below.

Luke 13:10–13
Luke 13:14
Luke 13:15
Luke 13:16
Luke 13:17

14. How is the Church like the mustard seed and the leaven? Luke 13:18–21

15. How will you enter heaven? Luke 13:22–24

16. Explain the parable in Luke 13:25–29.

17. What virtue does Luke 13:30 recommend?

18. Who warned Jesus about Herod? Luke 13:31–32

19. Did the warning deter Jesus? Luke 13:33

20. Why does Jesus go to Jerusalem? How does He feel about Jerusalem? Luke 13:33–35

* Describe some examples of people today who reject the idea of the *narrow door*.

Monthly Social Activity

This month, your small group will meet for coffee, tea, or a simple breakfast, lunch, or dessert in someone's home. Pray for this social event and for the host or hostess. Try, if at all possible, to attend.

My favorite parable is….

In this parable, I most identify with….

Some examples:

    — *The sower and the seed… I feel like good soil.*

    — *The widow's mite… I give what I can.*

    — *The prodigal son… I feel like the older brother.*

CHAPTER 13

Humility
Luke 14

For every one who exalts himself will be humbled,
and he who humbles himself will be exalted.
Luke 14:11

Humility is freedom from pride and arrogance, encompassing a modest and accurate assessment of one's own worth. Humility entails a deep sense of personal lowliness in contrast with God's supreme and perfect goodness. The perfect model of humility, of course, is Jesus. Saint Paul instructs believers to model Jesus' virtue of humility. *Have this mind among yourselves, which was in Christ Jesus, who though he was in the form of God, did not count equality with God a thing to be grasped, but emptied himself, taking the form of a servant, being born in the likeness of men. And being found in human form he humbled himself and became obedient unto death, even death on a cross* (Philippians 2:5–8). Jesus is our model.

False humility does not equate with virtue. God expects an honest appraisal of oneself. It does no good to pretend that gifts and talents do not exist. That is simply another form of hypocrisy, or play-acting. When paid a compliment, do not say, "Oh, it was nothing." That can draw even more attention to self. Rather, humility requires honest acceptance and gratitude. It would be preferable to say, "Thank you. May God be glorified," for after all, gifts and talents come from above.

Meals form an important setting in Luke's Gospel. Jesus enjoys opportunities to dine with others and often uses these opportunities to teach and preach. Similarly, in every society, the dinner table affords an opportunity for family and friends to sit down together, thank God for the food, and enjoy conversation and table fellowship. Children learn manners and values as they enter into conversation with parents, relatives, and other adults. Often there is laughter and compassion in sharing of the joys and trials of each person's day. Perhaps today, the evil one robs families of this simple pleasure of eating together because of the hectic pace and busyness of life.

Several meal settings emerge in Luke 14. *One sabbath when he went to dine at the house of a ruler who belonged to the Pharisees, they were watching him* (Luke 14:1). Note that Jesus dines with a ruler of the Pharisees. Here is the last time in Luke's Gospel that Jesus will face a controversy concerning the Sabbath. *And behold, there was a man before him who had dropsy* (Luke 14:2). Dropsy involved excessive fluid retention, with accompanying ascites and impaired circulation. The afflicted person suffered a swollen abdomen, with swelling in the arms and legs. Jesus shows compassion for the man's affliction, asking the lawyers and Pharisees, those who were responsible for interpreting the law, *"Is it lawful to heal on the sabbath, or not?"* But they were silent

(Luke 14:3). The question should be rhetorical. Jesus once again shows Himself to be the "Lord of the Sabbath," who shows compassion and performs miraculous deeds on the Lord's Day. The Father and the Son continue to work on the Sabbath.

Even though people are watching Jesus, waiting to trip Him up and accuse Him, Jesus does not change His behavior to appease or accommodate them. Jesus is the model for Christians. He obeys the Father's will and stays the course on the path to the Cross, notwithstanding the critical scrutiny of others. Jesus does the right thing, despite what the crowd does or expects. Jesus heals the man and then points out to the Pharisees that they take care of their beasts on the Sabbath. If an ox falls into a well, they will pull him out. Jesus knows that people are more important than animals, and that the Pharisees' and lawyers' interpretation of the law lacks consistency and compassion.

Blessed Solanus Casey (1870–1957) offers a wonderful example of humility and love for the sick and the poor. He was born the sixth of sixteen children in Wisconsin. After hearing God's call to the priesthood, he entered the diocesan seminary. At that time classes were taught in German and Latin, neither of which he understood. Therefore, he could not pass his classes. Later, he entered the Capuchin seminary. Although he was still a poor student, he was ordained a priest simplex—able to say Mass, but not permitted to preach homilies or hear confessions.

During the Great Depression, when many people were hungry, Father Solanus would go to the chapel to pray, and a truckload of bread would arrive for the soup kitchen. People came to the monastery in Detroit and told the humble doorkeeper their problems—troubled marriages, alcoholism, unemployment, and various sicknesses. Father Solanus prayed and many crosses were lightened.

On one occasion, a bricklayer suffered an industrial accident with lye burning his eyes. He was blinded in both eyes. His wife went to Father Solanus in tears, "We have five children. How will we survive? Who ever heard of a blind bricklayer?" Father Solanus told her to pray to Saint Joseph. When the ophthalmologists at Grace Hospital removed the bandages, they found two perfectly healed eyes!

Humility and hospitality—Jesus uses a parable concerning a wedding dinner, a familiar event in all cultures and times. Everyone enjoys a wedding celebration. People like to choose the best seats. No one wants to sit by the noisy kitchen doors. But sitting at the head table can prove embarrassing if the person must be asked to move. Jesus knows that the Pharisees and lawyers love to sit in the places of honor. Self-promotion does not impress or please God or others.

Luke uses the Greek term *kekl menoi* for "those invited" to refer to the elect, or those who consider themselves to be the chosen ones. The Pharisees and lawyers considered themselves to be "the elect." In contrast, Jesus issues an invitation to everyone. Jesus reaches out to Jews and Gentiles, men and women, the healthy and infirm, rich and poor, sinners and saints.

Most cultures have an expectation of reciprocity. When you are invited for dinner, you are expected to later repay your hosts with a reciprocal invitation. Jesus, once again, turns the table upside down. *But when you give a feast, invite the poor, the maimed, the lame, the blind, and you will be blessed, because they cannot repay you. You will be repaid at the resurrection of the just* (Luke 14:13–14). The early Church heeds Jesus' exhortation, and takes a concern for the widows and orphans, just as Jesus encouraged. The Catholic Church continues this practice of reaching out to the poor and sick some two thousand years later.

The great banquet—*Blessed is he who shall eat bread in the kingdom of God!* (Luke 14:15). What are believers waiting and hoping to enjoy? In the Book of Revelation, the angel tells John: *Blessed are those who are invited to the marriage supper of the Lamb* (Revelation 19:9). The eternal beatitude will be to enjoy table fellowship with the Blessed Trinity and the saints in the kingdom of heaven. All celebrations on earth will pale in comparison to the banquet in heaven.

The parable of the great banquet underscores the importance of responding to God's invitation and the seriousness of rejecting God's call. In this parable the invitation is offered three times, three excuses are given for not responding, and the servant is sent out three times. The moral of the story is that when God invites you to follow Him, pray for the grace to overcome any temptation or obstacle that stands in the way of accepting His invitation. *Compel people to come in* (Luke 14:23) should not be construed as advocating forced conversion. The Catholic Church has always believed that faith is free gift. The Church respects and honors free will. This statement presupposes urgency. Imagine that a person is contemplating suicide, preparing to leap from a bridge. You call the police and use any means necessary to try to save that person's life. Similarly, one should use all acceptable means to try to help save someone's eternal life—his soul.

The cost of discipleship—Here, Jesus uses oriental hyperbole—a figure of speech, which employs exaggeration or overstatement to make a point. Jesus has already commanded believers to love everyone, even enemies. God expects fulfillment of the commandment: *Honor your father and your mother, that your days may be long in the land which the LORD your God gives you* (Exodus 20:12). But just as Jesus demands detachment from material things, believers must also detach from everything, even good things like relationships. Nothing can take the place of singular devotion to God. Even good things—marriage, children, and careers can become idols.

C.S. Lewis wrote a fictional story about a group of people on their way to heaven. One woman said that if her son, who had predeceased her, was not in heaven, then, she did not want to go there either. Well, her son was in heaven, but the mother did not join him because her excessive devotion and inordinate attachment to her son had destroyed her relationship with God.

A real-life situation occurred in which a Catholic man's adult son stopped going to church and took up with some wayward women, causing a painful estrangement in the father-son relationship. The father prayed for his son, and said, "I would rather have my son hate me, but ultimately come to know the love and mercy of his Heavenly Father, than have my son love me but lose his immortal soul forever." This type of tough love requires courage and humility. Some people are so afraid of hurting another's feelings or losing friendships that they lack the courage to point out those mortal sins that can break one's relationship with God and jeopardize one's eternal salvation.

Whoever does not bear his own cross and come after me, cannot be my disciple (Luke 14:27). People must reflect on the call to discipleship. This is not a prosperity gospel—believe and everything will be sunshine and roses. Jesus tells the truth. Suffering comes to all people in this world, believers and unbelievers alike. Jesus embraces the Cross and invites disciples to do the same. The road to holiness demands believers to accept the various struggles, conflicts, and troubles that come their way. People will face financial reversals, health ailments, betrayals, or relationship problems. These are the trials and tribulations of human life. James tells us to count it all joy, because God can bring good out of suffering. *Blessed is the man who endures trial, for when he has stood the test he will receive the crown of life which God has promised to those who love him* (James 1:12). Jesus invites all of us to deny ourselves, take up the cross, and follow Him.

Jesus warns about a superficial discipleship that fails to take into account the cost that will be involved. Three examples show inadequate planning. A failed building project, a conquered king, and spoiled salt—all illustrate the sorry effects of failure to plan. Architects, rulers, and chefs all must evaluate whether they have what is necessary to complete the task and succeed. The disciple must do the same.

Believers must be diligent so that their commitment to Christ does not become weak or ineffective. Discipleship requires discipline. It takes discipline to embrace a small cross or a huge one. In order for a soul to be united with God, it must first detach itself from everything that could become an obstacle to union with God. Sin must go first. Then other inordinate attachments of the heart, even good things, must be released. God wants to give every good gift to His children. But in order to receive blessings from God, hands must be open. Clenched fists that cling to material things or relationships cannot accept supernatural gifts from above.

Jesus knew that His Apostles would follow Him and embrace martyrdom in many cases. He encourages them to count the cost and prepare. If we cannot deny ourselves in small ways, how would we ever have the courage to face martyrdom? It is in denying ourselves in small ways that we can prepare for a holy death.

Humility, hospitality, and discipleship emerge in Luke 14. These are attributes that every Christian will need to develop with God's grace and assistance. In doing so, the believer will be prepared for the great banquet in the kingdom to come.

A Humble Woman

Agnes Bojaxhiu was born on August 26, 1910 in Skopje, Macedonia, of Albanian heritage. She entered the convent of the Sisters of Loreto in Dublin, and took the name Teresa, after Saint Therese of Lisieux, the Little Flower. She was sent to India to teach in Saint Mary's Bengali School. Thereafter, the students called her Mother Teresa. In 1946, on a train journey from Calcutta to Darjeeling, Mother Teresa received what she described as "a call within a call" to care for the poorest of the poor, those dying on the streets of Calcutta.

Mother Teresa would go around the streets and hovels of Calcutta to pick up destitute, dying people. She would bring them to her House for the Dying, bathe their wounds, feed them soup, and care for them until death. Other women joined her order and volunteers also offered their help.

In 1950, a new religious order, the Missionaries of Charity, was officially recognized in the Archdiocese of Calcutta. The aim and mission of this order was to "quench the infinite thirst of Jesus on the cross for love and souls by laboring for the salvation and sanctification of the poorest of the poor."

Soon orphanages were opened to care for abandoned infants and children. Then, Mother Teresa opened hospices for people dying from AIDS. Homes for the dying were opened in over one hundred thirty countries. Today, there are almost five thousand Missionaries of Charity serving around the world.

In 1979 Mother Teresa was awarded the Nobel Prize. A lavish dinner usually accompanies the festivities to honor the recipient. Mother Teresa asked that they forego the dinner and instead give the money to the poor.

Ultimately, an order of Missionary of Charity priests and brothers evolved to embrace the call that Mother Teresa had heard from God, in her "call within a call." These priests and brothers bring the sacraments and embrace the vision of quenching the thirst of Christ by serving the poorest of the poor.

Mother Teresa became perhaps the most widely recognized woman in the world in the last century. Despite her virtue of humility, her photograph graced the front cover of many magazines. Even unbelievers marveled at her efforts, although she was not without her critics. She spoke at the United Nations General Assembly in 1985 and championed the cause of the poor, the neglected, the unwanted, and especially the vulnerable child in the womb.

Mother Teresa served tirelessly until her death. When sisters suggested that she rest, she replied that she would have plenty of time to rest in the next world. She died on September 5, 1997 and was beatified by Saint John Paul II.

Humility is the virtue that keeps within just limits the love of one's own excellence. Self-esteem often induces us to make ourselves too evident, or to occupy a place that is higher than our due. Humility keeps us *in our own place*. Humility is truth: it tends to establish in truth both our intellect—by making us know ourselves as we really are—and our life, by inclining us to take, in relation to God and to men, our proper place and no other.

Humility makes us realize that, in the sight of God, we are only His little creature, entirely dependent upon Him for our existence and for all our works. Having received life from God, we cannot subsist even one moment independently of Him.

Father Gabriel of Saint Mary Magdalen, OCD, *Divine Intimacy* (London: Baronius Press, 2008), 304

1. What happens in Luke 14:1–4?

2. Find a common issue with each of the healings in these passages.

Luke 6:1–5
Luke 6:6–11
Luke 13:10–16

3. What does Jesus ask of the lawyers and Pharisees? Luke 14:5

4. How do the lawyers and Pharisees respond? Luke 14:6

5. Outline the parable of the wedding feast.

Luke 14:7–8a
Luke 14:8b–9
Luke 14:10a
Luke 14:10b

6. What is the moral of the story? Luke 14:11

7. Explain the virtue of humility.

8. How could you grow in this virtue? Matthew 20:26–28

* Explain the difference between true and false humility.

9. To whom is Jesus speaking in Luke 14:12?

10. Outline Jesus' instructions regarding offering hospitality.

Luke 14:12	
Luke 14:13	
Luke 14:14a	

* Have you ever offered hospitality to someone who could not reciprocate? Explain.

11. When should a Christian expect a reward? Luke 14:14b

12. What can you learn from these verses?

Luke 14:15	
Revelation 19:9	

** When can you enjoy the Supper of the Lord?

13. What happens in the following verses?

Luke 14:16–17
Luke 14:21
Luke 14:23

14. What excuses are given for refusing to come to the banquet?

Luke 14:18
Luke 14:19
Luke 14:20

* What excuses do people give today for not coming to the Eucharist?

15. What results from refusing God's invitation? Luke 14:24

16. What can result from refusing to obey Christ's commands? Matthew 25:41–46

17. Explain the cost of discipleship. Luke 14:26–27

18. Identify three examples of lack of preparedness.

Luke 14:28–30
Luke 14:31–32
Luke 14:34–35

19. Ultimately, what is required to be a disciple of Jesus?

Luke 14:33
Philippians 3:7–8

20. Recall an example of true humility in Luke's Gospel. Luke 7:4–9

* Identify some examples of humility in contemporary culture.

** Share some practical ways to grow in the virtue of humility.

Chapter 14

The Prodigal Son
Luke 15

I tell you, there is joy before the angels of God over one sinner who repents. . . .
"It was fitting to make merry and be glad,
for this your brother was dead, and is alive; he was lost, and is found."
Luke 15:10, 32

The Prodigal Son, according to Mark Twain, is the best short story ever written. Jesus told this story to His listeners, and Luke wrote it down for people to enjoy, consider, and meditate upon centuries later. The parable of the Prodigal Son appears only here in the Gospel of Luke. This short story of only two paragraphs, or twenty-one verses, may actually be the story of every man and every woman. Look closely and you will find yourself in the parables of Jesus.

Jesus tells three stories of loss and mercy: a lost sheep, lost money, and two lost sons. Two short parallel parables are followed by a longer parable that has the same moral to the story. Luke's parallel structure illustrates the technique of a highly effective communicator—Jesus, the Master Storyteller.

> **Mercy**—benevolence, compassion, or tenderness of heart,
> disposing one to overlook wrongs,
> or to treat an offender better than he or she deserves.

Luke's parable of the lost sheep is also told in Matthew's Gospel (18:12–14). This parable anticipates Jesus' identification of Himself as the Good Shepherd, who lays down His life for His sheep (John 10:1ff). *Just so, I tell you, there will be more joy in heaven over one sinner who repents than over ninety-nine righteous persons who need no repentance* (Luke 15:7). This verse does not imply that God is not pleased with the faithfulness and perseverance of righteous believers, but that He greatly desires to seek out the lost. Today's Church spends the bulk of its time and resources on the ninety-nine—the faithful. Very little energy and resources are expended on going out after the lost, the fallen away, the disgruntled, and those who desperately need to taste God's mercy and forgiveness. What can we do to reach out to the lost?

Jesus speaks about both men and women. Luke recounts the first parable involving a man who loses a sheep. The second parable deals with a woman who loses money. The coin was a *drachma*, equivalent to about one day's wage for a worker. "Speaking more obscurely in the parable of the silver coin, he tells us that the purpose of his coming was to reclaim the royal image, which had become coated with the filth of sin," says Saint Maximus the Confessor (*Letter*, 11). Contemporary people can identify with losing money—a wallet, purse, or credit card. Great relief and rejoicing follow when lost money or possessions are found.

Prodigal—given to extravagant expenditures,
profuse, lavish, wasteful, spendthrift.

God is a prodigal father, lavishing gifts on children who do not deserve His love. His mercy and love are profuse and extravagant. *For as the heavens are high above the earth, so great is his mercy toward those who fear him; as far as the east is from the west, so far does he remove our transgressions from us. . . . The mercy of the* LORD *is from everlasting to everlasting upon those who fear him* (Psalm 103:11–12, 17). God lavishes love and forgiveness on sinners from generation to generation.

Pope Emeritus Benedict XVI reveals that the parable of the prodigal son could just as easily be called "The Parable of the Good Father," or "The Parable of the Two Brothers." Sibling rivalry appears repeatedly in the Bible, and it continues throughout history across cultures. The very first two brothers in the Old Testament, Cain and Abel, get off to a very bad start (Genesis 4). Esau and Jacob start battling even in their mother's womb (Genesis 25:21ff). Joseph and his brothers experience favoritism issues and jealousy (Genesis 37).

Matthew recounts a parable of two brothers who are asked by their father to go work in the vineyard. The first refuses, but later repents, and obeys his father. The second son agrees promptly, but fails to follow through, and does not honor his word. Jesus asks: *Which of the two did the will of his father?* (Matthew 21:31). Jesus attempts to communicate the relationship between the Pharisees and public sinners. Repentant tax collectors and harlots are receiving God's mercy, while the self-righteous refuse to see their sin and their need for forgiveness. God is not like us. The Gospels surprise us by looking at life through God's eyes.

In the parable of the prodigal son, the term "justice" is not used even once; just as in the original text the term "mercy" is not used either. Nevertheless, the relationship between justice and love, that is manifested as mercy, is inscribed with great exactness in the content of the Gospel parable. It becomes more evident that love is transformed into mercy when it is necessary to go beyond the precise norm of justice—precise and often too narrow. . . . The father of the prodigal son is faithful to his fatherhood, faithful to the love that he had always lavished on his son.

Saint John Paul II, Encyclical Letter Rich in Mercy *Dives in Misericordia* (November 30, 1980), 5.6, 6.1

The younger son in this parable begins by exhibiting arrogance and selfishness. *Father, give me the share of property that falls to me* (Luke 15:12). The son does not wait to receive a gift that is offered. He does not wait to receive his inheritance until after the death of his father, but demands immediate gratification of his desires. It appears as if the young son values money over relationships. Nevertheless, the father gives in to his request and grants his son total freedom, the freedom to mess up his life. The young son's journey into a far country represents humanity's descent into sin. Contemporary people can identify with going far afield and ending up in a place they never imagined. Sin is seductive and always enslaves. Ultimately, the young son hits the bottom of his barrel. Often people must come to the end of their rope before they can reach out to God for redemption.

When the son comes to his senses, he realizes that his father's slaves are better off than he is. Hunger and loneliness represent the soul estranged from God. The young man shows heartfelt repentance and confession. *I will arise and go to my father, and I will say to him, "Father, I have sinned against heaven and before you; I am no longer worthy to be called your son; treat me as one of your hired servants"* (Luke 15:18–19). Similarly, when we hit rock bottom and then come to our senses, the path to return to the Father's house comes through the Sacrament of Reconciliation.

The father waits for his son. God thirsts and longs for the sinner's return. *How can I give you up, O Ephraim! How can I hand you over, O Israel! . . . My heart recoils within me, my compassion grows warm and tender. I will not execute my fierce anger . . . for I am God and not man, the Holy One in your midst, and I will not come to destroy* (Hosea 11:8–9). When the prodigal returns, his father runs to him. Men in ancient Israel did not run. Children ran. Servants ran. Slaves ran. Prominent men sat and waited for others to wait on them. The father shows great humility in running out to meet his wayward son. He shows lavish generosity in restoring him to his place in the family and celebrating his return. Similarly, God shows great humility in reaching out to sinners and showing mercy and forgiveness.

Ironically, the father in this parable has two lost sons. The elder son demonstrates anger and resentment, priding himself on being the "good son." Self-righteousness and pride can block one from receiving God's mercy and love. His heart is hard and cold. The older son wants justice for his brother, not mercy. He is not relieved to see his brother come home, healthy and unharmed. His younger brother could have died in the far country, but the older brother does not care. He wants vengeance. Just like the Pharisees, the elder brother looks good on the outside, but on the inside he seethes with self-righteous indignation and bitterness.

The parable of the prodigal son ends with a cliffhanger. What will happen to this family? Will the older brother cool off and come to the party? Will the two brothers reconcile? Find yourself in this story. Are you like the father—lavish in mercy and love? Are you more like the older brother—angry, bitter, self-righteous, and resentful? Have you behaved like the younger son—selfish, foolish, and sinful, but repentant? Are you grateful for God's mercy for yourself and others? The most beautiful exegesis on this parable comes from Pope Benedict XVI.

The Parable of the Two Brothers

The son squanders his inheritance. He just wants to enjoy himself. He wants to scoop life out till there is nothing left. He wants to have "life in abundance" as he understands it. He no longer wants to be subject to any commandment, any authority. He seeks radical freedom. He wants to live only for himself, free of any other claim. He enjoys life; he feels that he is completely autonomous.

Is it difficult for us to see clearly reflected here the spirit of the modern rebellion against God and God's law? . . . At the end it is all gone. He who was once completely free is now truly a slave. Those who understand freedom as the radically arbitrary license to do just what they want and to have their own way are living a lie, for by his very nature man is part of a shared existence and his freedom is shared freedom. . . . A false autonomy leads to slavery. . . . The totally free man has become a wretched slave.

At this point the "conversion" takes place. The prodigal son realizes that he is lost—that at home he was free and that his father's servants are freer than he now is, who had once considered himself completely free. . . . His change of heart, his "conversion" consists in his recognition of this, his realization that he has become alienated and wandered into truly "alien lands," and his return to himself. . . . He is on a pilgrimage toward the truth of his existence, and that means "homeward". . . .

The father "sees the son from far off" and goes out to meet him. He listens to the son's confession and perceives in it the interior journey that he has made; he perceives that the son has found the way to true freedom. . . .

The Church Fathers put all their love into the exposition of this scene. The lost son they take as an image of man as such, of "Adam," who all of us are—of Adam whom God has gone out to meet and whom he has received anew into his house. In the parable, the father orders the servants to bring quickly "the first robe." For the [Church] Fathers, this "first robe" is a reference to the lost robe of grace with which man had been originally clothed, but which he forfeited by sin. But now this "first robe" is given back to him—the robe of the son. The feast that is now made ready they read as an image of the feast of faith, the festive Eucharist, in which the eternal festal banquet is anticipated.

But the kernel of the text surely does not lie in these details; the kernel is now unmistakably the figure of the father. Can we understand him? . . . Because God is God, the Holy One, he acts as no man could act. . . . God's heart transforms wrath and turns punishment into forgiveness.

Pope Benedict XVI, *Jesus of Nazareth*
(New York: Doubleday, 2007), 203–207

1. Explain the parable in Luke 15:1–6.

2. What can you learn about helping a sinner to repent?

Luke 15:7
Ephesians 4:15
James 5:20

* Have you ever had the courage to confront a sinner, speaking the truth in love?

3. Who is the protagonist in the parable in Luke 15:8–9?

4. How does the woman react when she finds her silver coin? Luke 15:9

** Have you ever lost something really valuable, like your way or your faith?

5. Compare the following verses.

Luke 15:7
Luke 15:10

6. Identify some pairs of troubled brothers in the Bible.

Genesis 4:1–9
Genesis 25:27–34
Genesis 37:1–4

7. Outline the beginning of the parable.

Luke 15:11–12
Luke 15:13
Luke 15:14–16
Luke 15:17–20a

8. What was the father doing? Luke 15:20b

9. What needs to happen to receive the Father's mercy?

Luke 15:21
CCC 1847
CCC 1848

10. What does the father do? Luke 15:20b, 22–24

11. What does the father recognize in his sons? CCC 1700

12. What is the significance of returning to the father's house? CCC 2795

13. How can someone return to the Father's house?

Acts 3:19
CCC 1455

14. How often must a Catholic go to Confession? CCC 1457

15. Where was the older brother? Luke 15:25

16. What did the servant tell the older son? Luke 15:27

17. How did the old brother react to his brother's return? Luke 15:28

18. What does the older son say to his father? Luke 15:29–30

19. What can you learn from these verses?

Luke 15:24	
Luke 15:32	
Ephesians 2:1	

20. What does the older son call his brother? Luke 15:30

* Where can you find yourself in the story? Where have you been in the past?

God or Mammon
Luke 16

No servant can serve two masters;
for either he will hate the one and love the other,
or he will be devoted to the one and despise the other.
You cannot serve God and mammon.
Luke 16:13

"**M**oney, money, money . . . it's a rich man's world," sings the Swedish pop group Abba. Is it so? Luke 16 has a great deal to say about money, looking at wealth from several different perspectives and angles. Luke begins by relaying a parable that Jesus told about a dishonest steward, who falsifies financial records and changes people's bills in order to ingratiate himself with the debtors. Next, there is mention of *unrighteous mammon* (Luke 16:11). What should one do about money that is stolen or gained by illicit means? What about drug money? Then, Jesus warns that you cannot serve God and money. You must choose. Jesus accuses the Pharisees of being *lovers of money* (Luke 16:14), not a compliment in the least. Finally, Jesus gives a parable about a rich man and the poor beggar Lazarus. These scenarios provide ample food for thought about the use and abuse of money.

The parable of the dishonest steward presents a rather confusing story. What is the point? At first read, it can almost seem as if dishonesty is being praised. But, the *master* speaking to his cunning steward refers to the *employer* in the story, not to Jesus, the Master. See the parallel of the younger son squandering his inheritance in the parable of the prodigal son (Luke 15:14) and the steward badly mismanaging his employer's finances and *wasting his goods* (Luke 16:1) in the parable of the dishonest steward. The steward then displays a radically ingenious way of preparing for his termination. Jesus assumes that everyone recognizes the immorality of the steward's sin. He does not praise dishonesty or wasteful behavior, but rather directs the disciples to observe the clever and industrious actions of the wicked. If evil people can be shrewd and inventive in worldly affairs, why are Christians so dull and lazy concerning the things of the kingdom?

Jesus tells the Apostles: *Behold, I send you out as sheep in the midst of wolves; so be wise as serpents and innocent as doves* (Matthew 10:16). Disciples must be wise and shrewd to advance the kingdom of God in the world. If worldly people can be clever and industrious in business enterprises to accumulate wealth, how much more should religious people invest creative energy and work diligently in order to attain moral character and virtue? Believers must also be imaginative and creative in proclaiming the Gospel and advancing God's kingdom of peace, justice, and mercy. The devil and his minions work hard from many angles. Christians must pray and work even harder and smarter to attain true riches and to evangelize others.

A practical application of Jesus' admonition can be seen in the explosion of creative, fresh, new ideas for evangelism. Catholic television and radio programs, home Bible studies, neighborhood groups, theology on tap lectures in bars, door-to-door evangelism, vacation Bible schools for children, outreaches to teens, young adults, singles, married couples, families, the elderly, the widowed, the separated and divorced—all fall outside the box. Christian concerts featuring rap or rock music with a Gospel message reach out to the un-churched and those in need of God's mercy and love. Full-length movies depict the life of Christ, biblical themes, or subtle Gospel values. Many lay-initiated endeavors succeed in advancing the kingdom of God in ingenious and imaginative new ways. You may be involved in some of these efforts, and you probably have some clever new ideas as well.

True riches refer to heavenly capital. Unrighteous mammon, stolen or ill-gotten goods, must be returned and restitution made. Disciples must use the mammon of this world in ways that please God. Almsgiving and care for the hungry, the poor, and the needy are excellent uses for capital. The evil one can use mammon to seduce believers away from God. Believers should detach from material things and cling to God. Jesus never said that wealth is evil. He has affluent friends, like Joseph of Arimathea and various women, who are good and generous. Only craving for wealth, or misuse of money, gets people into trouble. You cannot serve God and money.

> **Mammon**—riches, wealth,
> or the god of riches.

The love of money—Luke reveals that the Pharisees were lovers of money. Money is not evil in itself, but Saint Paul warns us: *the love of money is the root of all evils; it is through this craving that some have wandered away from the faith* (1 Timothy 6:10). Jesus again confronts the Pharisees. *You are those who justify yourselves before men, but God knows your hearts; for what is exalted among men is an abomination in the sight of God* (Luke 16:15). The use of money in the Church and by Christians can alleviate the suffering of many. But money continues to present challenges, and misuse of funds can cause great scandal.

Marriage is a lifelong covenant between a man and a woman, ordered to the well-being of the spouses and the procreation and education of children. Jesus reiterates God's initial intent in designing marriage as a faithful covenant of love between one man and one woman for life. *Have you not read that he who made them from the beginning made them male and female, and said, "For this reason a man shall leave his father and mother and be joined to his wife, and the two shall become one"? . . . What therefore God has joined together, let no man put asunder* (Matthew 19:4–6). Matthew expands Jesus' words more fully than Luke, who concisely warns against divorce: *Every one who divorces his wife and marries another commits adultery* (Luke 16:18). Faithful marriage—one man with one woman for life—is God's ideal.

The parable of the rich man and Lazarus—In this parable the rich man is nameless, but the poor beggar Lazarus has the Latin form of the Hebrew name *Eleazar*, which means "God has helped me." This name is similar to that of Abraham's servant, Eliezer of Damascus, who Abram planned to make his heir (Genesis 15:2). Note that no sins of commission are evident in the life of the rich man. The text does not reveal that the rich man lied, cheated, stole, or murdered anyone. But his chief sin seems to be a sin of "omission." He refused to see the poor man who lay at his gate sick, hungry, and in need. He failed to practice any corporal works of mercy.

There was a rich man, who was clothed in purple and fine linen and who feasted sumptuously every day. And at his gate lay a poor man named Lazarus, full of sores, who desired to be fed with what fell from the rich man's table (Luke 16:19–20). But Lazarus received nothing. We can be oblivious to the poor and the hungry in our midst. They can become invisible to us as we go about our business.

> Why do sinners have an abundance of wealth and riches, and feast constantly and sumptuously, knowing no pain or sorrow, while the just are in want and are punished by the loss of spouse or children? The parable in the Gospel must supply the answer. The rich man was clothed in purple and fine linen and gave great banquets every day; but the poor man, full of sores, gathered the crumbs from his table. After the death of each of them, however, the poor man took his rest in the bosom of Abraham, while the rich man was in torment. Is it not evident from this that rewards and punishments according to merits await us after death?
> Saint Ambrose of Milan (333–339), *The Duties of the Clergy*, 1, 15, 57

People in Jesus' time believed that riches proved that wealthy people were holy and righteous, and thus blessed by God. Conversely, they thought that illness and poverty were just punishments for sin. So, if you were sick or hungry, you deserved it because you were lazy, a sinner, or your parents were sinners. But Jesus turns the table on such wrong-headed notions. Nowhere does Jesus condemn the possession of riches, but He warns against using wealth in a selfish way, without concern for others. Who will you serve—God and neighbor, or self and money? Many people have savings accounts and investment plans to insure their material security in this life. But how many people invest in the world to come—eternal life?

The tables turn for Lazarus and the rich man. On earth, Lazarus was in torment and the rich man feasted sumptuously every day. But death comes to all people. Death is the great leveler of the rich and the poor. *The poor man died and was carried by the angels to Abraham's bosom. The rich man also died and was buried; and in Hades, being in torment, he lifted up his eyes, and saw Abraham far off and Lazarus in his bosom* (Luke 16:22–23). Every person, rich and poor, will one day die and be buried, and then give an accounting of his or her life. The good that can be done must be done now, not later. Tomorrow is not promised to anyone.

> Riches and freedom mean a special responsibility. Riches and freedom create a special obligation. And so, in the name of the solidarity that binds us all together in a common humanity, I again proclaim the dignity of every human person: the rich man and Lazarus are both human beings, both of them equally created in the image and likeness of God, both of them equally redeemed by Christ, at a great price, the price of the *precious blood of Christ* (1 Peter 1:19).
>
> Saint John Paul II, *Homily,* October 2, 1979

Now, the rich man who ignored Lazarus in this world wants Abraham to make Lazarus come to his assistance in Hades. The rich man remains a narcissist. He is in torment and he does not like it one bit, having been accustomed to luxurious living and servants waiting on him. He could afford his comfort. He, who would not help a fellow human being in need, now expects to receive help. But, what goes around comes around. Kindness often returns to the person who showed kindness. Indifference can be repaid with indifference and diffidence.

There is a great chasm between this world and the next. Most people who have experienced the death of a loved one understand that great chasm. The beloved who spoke and listened and laughed yesterday, speaks no more. Silence looms between earth and the grave, between the living and the dead. Until the next world, interaction is broken. And another chasm exists between heaven and hell. So, it is of utmost importance to consider carefully our actions in this life. Repent now.

> I beseech you and entreat you, that so long as we have this tenuous grasp on life we might be sorely pricked by what has been said, that we might be converted and become better persons; that we may not, like that rich man, lament to no purpose when we have gone hence, and continue in incurable lamentation. For even if you have a father, even if you have a son, even if you have a friend, even if you have any person at all who has ready speech with God, none of these shall ever save you when you have been condemned by your own works. . . . For if we have been remiss, no just man will assist us—no prophet, no apostle, no one at all.
>
> Saint John Chrysostom (344–407), *Homilies,* 42, 3, 5

Today is the time to share riches. Never wait to become rich to feed the hungry. Even the materially poor, like the widow (Luke 21:2–3), can share something. Everyone, even children, can give alms. Performing spiritual and corporal works of mercy must be done now, not at some future date that may never come. The time to become creative and industrious in sharing the Gospel is now. Jesus warns His listeners in the first century and readers today that life is short. There will be an accounting. As radically clever as the dishonest steward was, you can be even more ingenious and energetic in advancing the kingdom of God by honest and creative means.

A Lavishly Generous Debutante

Katharine Drexel, the second daughter of Francis Drexel, a wealthy Philadelphia banker, was born on November 26, 1858. She was educated privately at home and travelled widely throughout the United States and Europe. Katharine made her social debut in 1879 and enjoyed many suitors. However, her heart was drawn to the plight of Native Americans and African Americans.

When Francis Drexel died in 1885, he left a $15.5 million estate to his daughters. (In current currency, his estate would be worth approximately $400 million). To prevent his daughters from falling prey to fortune hunters, Francis crafted his will so that his daughters controlled the income from his estate, and on their deaths any remaining inheritance would go to grandchildren or revert to living sisters.

At a private audience with Pope Leo XIII in 1887, Katharine asked for missionaries to staff the Indian missions that she was financing. The Pope surprised Katharine by asking her to become a missionary herself. Although she had received marriage proposals, and her uncle tried to dissuade her, her spiritual director Bishop James O'Connor encouraged her in pursuing religious life. She entered the Sisters of Mercy, and later, Mother Katharine established a new order, the Sisters of the Blessed Sacrament, to minister to Native Americans and African Americans.

She established fifty missions for Native Americans and a system of African American Catholic schools in thirteen states, plus sixty missions and rural schools. Despite harassment from the Ku Klux Klan, she established Xavier University in New Orleans, the first such institution of higher education predominantly for African Americans in the United States.

In Texas, Klansmen posted a sign on the door of a church where Blessed Sacrament Sisters had opened a school: "Stop services or flogging with tar and feathers will start." The Sisters started praying. A few days later, a violent thunderstorm destroyed the local Klan headquarters. Segregationists burned a school in Pennsylvania and vandals smashed every window in Xavier Preparatory School in New Orleans, but Mother Drexel was undaunted. She persevered and pressed on.

Over the course of sixty years, Mother Drexel spent $20 million of her private fortune building schools, churches, and a university, as well as paying the salaries of teachers in rural schools for African Americans and Native Americans. She outlived both of her sisters and died at the age of ninety-six on March 3, 1955.

Saint John Paul II canonized Mother Katharine Drexel on October 1, 2000. Saint Katharine Drexel's feast day is March 3. She provides a beautiful example of lavish generosity and money well spent by an extremely wealthy person.

1. Explain the parable of the dishonest steward. Luke 16:1–8

2. For which virtue did the master commend his steward?

Proverbs 8:5
Luke 16:8
CCC 1806

3. Define "prudence."

* How could one grow in the virtue of prudence?

4. Explain Luke 16:10–11 in your own words.

** What are some creative, clever ways to advance the kingdom of God?

5. What are "true riches"?

Luke 12:33b–34
Luke 16:11
Matthew 6:20

6. What are some things the Bible and Catechism say about money?

Proverbs 11:24
Ecclesiastes 5:10
Sirach 5:1
Sirach 31:5
Luke 16:13
1 Timothy 6:10
CCC 2424
CCC 2425

* How much time do you spend thinking or worrying about money?

7. What does God know?

Luke 16:14
Luke 16:15
1 Samuel 16:7
Proverbs 21:2
Acts 1:24

* What do you see in a person who has a good and generous heart?

8. Explain Luke 16:16–17.

9. What does Jesus reaffirm?

Genesis 2:24
Matthew 19:4–6
Luke 16:18
CCC 2381–2382

10. Describe the characters in the parable of the rich man and Lazarus.

Rich man–Luke 16:19
Lazarus–Luke 16:20
Angels–CCC 336
Abraham–Luke 16:22

11. What happens after death to Lazarus, hopefully?

Luke 16:22
Luke 16:25
CCC 633
CCC 1023–1024

12. What happens after death to the rich man, most probably?

Luke 16:22b–23
CCC 1021
CCC 1022, 1033

13. Describe the rich man's torment. Luke 16:23–24

14. What does the rich man ask Abraham? Luke 16:24

15. How does Abraham respond? Luke 16:25

16. What exists between earth and the beyond? Luke 16:26

17. What more does the rich man ask? Luke 16:27–28

18. How does Abraham respond? Luke 16:29

19. Is the rich man persistent? Luke 16:30

20. What is Abraham's final word? Luke 16:31

CHAPTER 16

The Kingdom of God
Luke 17

The kingdom of God is not coming with signs to be observed;
nor will they say, "Behold, here it is!" or "There!"
for behold, the kingdom of God is in your midst.
Luke 17:20–21

Temptations—*And he said to his disciples, "Temptations to sin are sure to come; but woe to him by whom they come! It would be better for him if a millstone were hung round his neck and he were cast into the sea, than that he should cause one of these little ones to sin"* (Luke 17:1–2). Matthew 18:6–7 and Mark 9:42 issue the same warnings. The little one could be a child or a new believer. In either case, to lead another into sin is itself a serious sin and carries grave consequences.

> It is necessary that scandals come. . . . But, when He speaks of it being necessary, He does not mean that the faculty of free will nor the ability of freely choosing is taken away, nor that life is made subject to some kind of necessity through the circumstances. He is only saying beforehand what will surely be. . . . It is not that His prediction brings the scandals. Away with such a notion! It is not because He foretold it that it happens; but because it surely must happen He did foretell it. If those who introduce scandals had not wanted to do such wickedness, the scandals would not have come; and if the scandals were not going to come, He would not have foretold them.
>
> Saint John Chrysostom (344–407), *Homilies, 59, 1*

A scandal is a stumbling block, something that causes people to fall. Scandal brings shame, confusion, dishonor, infamy, and disgrace. Sin disfigures, spoils, and violates another person, often an innocent young person. Sins perpetrated by adults in authority upon innocent children are the most heinous of crimes.

The basalt millstone, common in Israel in Jesus' time, weighed hundreds of pounds, had a hole in the middle, and was used for grinding grain. It would cause certain death by drowning for a sinner thrown into the sea. However, the spiritual, eternal death of the soul is far more serious than physical death. The process of temptation and falling into sin can be studied and avoided.

➤ Temptation begins with a subtle invitation to sin. The person knows right from wrong objectively, but begins to waver. Did God really say that? Surely, this one time can't hurt. I deserve this. I was born this way. I can't help it.

- Emotions and appetites distort and veil the seriousness of the act. How can it be wrong if it feels so right? Feelings cloud mature judgment and moral principles. A person becomes enchanted with anticipated forbidden pleasure.

- Decision follows. A good conscience enables one to overcome the temptation to sin. A poorly formed conscience or a weak will succumbs to the passions. Now, the decision to sin becomes sin. A man and woman planning to commit adultery but being thwarted have already sinned in their hearts.

- Evil action results. The internal decision to suppress the conscience takes on a visible form, and a sinful action usually follows. The sin of desire on the inside becomes the actual sin, and temptation finds its fulfillment.

- Habitual wrongdoing ensues. Sin never satisfies, but always craves more. Innocence fades and the individual becomes convinced that the sinful life is normal. Repentance and conversion become more remote.

- Bondage by the evil one results. A heart becomes hardened. The person feels driven to sin rather than to virtue. The person now becomes trapped in sin. Only Our Savior can liberate this soul from captivity.

- Choose hell or heaven. Clinging to sin until one's final breath seals the compact with wickedness forever and evil wins. Rejecting God's love and mercy on earth plunges the soul into eternal suffering. Only repentance, confession, and conversion can free the soul from darkness and restore it to God's mercy and love. Heaven awaits repentant sinners.

Rebuke sinners and forgive them—*Take heed to yourselves; if your brother sins, rebuke him, and if he repents, forgive him* (Luke 17:3). Confronting sin is not very popular in the contemporary culture of relativism. Who are you to judge? That might be right for you, but never impose your values on me. The only remaining virtue seems to be tolerance, especially the tolerance of sin and evil. But Jesus reiterates what the prophets declared. *If I say to the wicked, O wicked man, you shall surely die, and you do not speak to warn the wicked to turn from his way, that wicked man shall die in his iniquity, but his blood I will require at your hand. But if you warn the wicked to turn from his way, and he does not turn from his way; he shall die in his iniquity, but you will have saved your life* (Ezekiel 33:8–9). Confronting sin requires courage.

"With outstretched arms He begs us to turn toward Him, to weep for our sins, and to become servants of love, first for ourselves, then for our neighbor. Just as water extinguishes a fire, so love wipes out sin," wrote Saint John of God (*Letters*, 23). What incentive do you have for rebuking a sinner? *My brethren, if any one among you wanders from the truth and some one brings him back, let him know that whoever brings back a sinner from the error of his way will save his soul from death and cover a multitude of sins* (James 5:19–20). Do you want to save your soul from death? Would you like to cover over your multitude of sins? Bring back a sinner.

How does one rebuke a sinner? Paul encourages believers to *speak the truth in love* (Ephesians 4:15). This concept of rebuking a sinner in love may seem foreign and almost impossible to do. Sinners do not often respond to a rebuke with gratitude or immediate repentance and conversion. Anticipate anger and a negative reaction. Yet, Jesus calls believers to rebuke the one who sins. How can anyone receive the grace to repent if everyone is silent, accepting and tolerating sinful behavior as fine and normal? If a loved one fell asleep in a burning house, would you go in and drag him out? What one is willing to do to rescue a physical body should also be done for the eternal soul. Everlasting torment in hell is far worse than a house fire. Who will have the courage to tell sinners the truth? Don't pretend that sin is acceptable.

And if he repents, forgive him; and if he sins against you seven times in the day, and turns to you seven times, and says, "I repent," you must forgive him (Luke 17:3–4). God's mercy is inexhaustible. He forgives us, and we must forgive in return. However, the admonition above does not give license to endure abuse. Sometimes a loved one is forgiven, but cannot remain in the home for the safety and protection of others. An alcoholic or drug addict who repents but keeps on drinking or using drugs, and then beats the children while in a drunken stupor, should be forgiven and the locks changed. Cheap grace and cheap mercy do not often transform lives. Genuine repentance and conversion, and genuine forgiveness, bring about change. Forgiveness does not mean enabling sinful behavior to continue unchecked.

The apostles said to the Lord, "Increase our faith!" And the Lord said, "If you had faith as a grain of a mustard seed, you could say to this sycamine tree, 'Be rooted up, and be planted in the sea,' and it would obey you" (Luke 17:5–6). This sycamine tree resembles the mulberry, a large tree with an extensive root system, which would be hard to uproot and impossible to sustain in the sea. Just a little bit of faith can go a long way. If a person acts on faith, more faith will be given. The disciples of Jesus must be obedient in small things and then they will see miracles. The twelve Apostles start out as a small group, which will grow into a Catholic Church numbering over 1.2 billion souls on earth.

The parable of the servant who comes in from the field shows that everything we have—life, breath, sustenance, material comforts, faith—comes from God. We are God's unworthy servants. God's graciousness to us remains purely a gift. Humanity is always indebted to God. No matter what a person does for God or for others, that person can never repay God for all of the gifts received.

Jesus heals ten lepers—On His way to Jerusalem Jesus passes near Samaria, where He encounters ten lepers who beg, *Jesus, Master, have mercy on us* (Luke 17:12). The actual healing event is not described in the text, but Jesus tells them to show themselves to the priest, following the prescription in Mosaic Law for lepers who had been cleansed. Only one of the lepers returns to thank Jesus. What happened to the other nine? One can only imagine. Perhaps a husband and father among the lepers was so excited to rejoin his family that he ran home. Perhaps another leper was too frightened or shy to approach Jesus. *Then one of them, when he saw that he was healed, turned back, praising God* *with a loud voice; and he fell on his face at Jesus' feet, giving him thanks* (Luke 17:15–16). The foreigner, the Samaritan, returns to Jesus, which reveals his conversion, and he praises and worships God in the most humble of postures. Luke frequently uses this term *praising God* (Luke 2:20; 5:25, 26; 7:16; 13:13; 18:43; 23:47; Acts 4:21; 21:20) as people respond to divine manifestations of mercy and power.

Thanksgiving—Jesus makes a point. *Was no one found to return and give praise to God except this foreigner?* (Luke 17:18). Thanksgiving is the expected human response to a blessing. Even small children learn to say "thank you" for the food, sweets, or gifts they receive. Serving in a soup kitchen, the most wounded souls are those who can no longer express gratitude. The words "thank" and "thanks" appear in the Bible one hundred fifty times. These are extremely important words for the Christian to repeat frequently. Psychiatrists indicate that a person cannot be both miserable and grateful at the same time. So, if you are miserable, develop an attitude of gratitude and your spirits may improve. A grateful heart is not prone to sin.

Ann Voskamp, a Mennonite wife and mother living on a pig farm in Canada, wrote a *New York Times* best-selling book called *One Thousand Gifts*. She describes her challenge in writing down one thousand things for which she was grateful and how this endeavor changed her life. She dares others to live fully, right where they are. Thanksgiving, whether oral or written down, blesses relationships. Loved ones are blessed by expressions of gratitude. God deserves thanks and praise.

The Coming of the Kingdom—Many Jews expect the kingdom of God to involve political elimination of forces hostile to the Jews. They do not recognize that the kingdom of God comes in the person of Jesus. Jesus exhorts the disciples to remain faithful during difficult times of persecution until He comes again in glory. False prophets will arise, but the disciples will not follow them. The Lord's Second Coming will be sudden and unexpected. Just as in the times of Noah (Genesis 6:9ff) and Lot (Genesis 18:16ff), many people will be unprepared for divine judgment.

The Second Coming of Christ will usher in the last judgment on all of humanity. Jesus warns the disciples of false prophets and persecutions preceding His return in glory. *Immediately after the tribulation of those days the sun will be darkened, and the moon will not give its light, and the stars will fall from heaven, and the powers of the heavens will be shaken; then will appear the sign of the Son of man in heaven, and then all the tribes of the earth will mourn, and they will see the Son of man coming on the clouds of heaven with power and great glory; and he will send out his angels with a loud trumpet call, and they will gather his elect from the four winds, from one end of heaven to the other* (Matthew 24:29–31). Luke uses examples of both men and women to indicate that some men and some women will find favor with God, and others will wait too long. *For you yourselves know well that the day of the Lord will come like a thief in the night* (1 Thessalonians 5:2). Therefore, with a prayerful, thankful heart, be prepared to meet the Lord. He may come sooner than you think.

An Act of Thanksgiving

Muzyad Yakhoob was born January 6, 1912 in Deerfield, Michigan, one of ten children in a Lebanese Catholic family. He dropped out of high school in his freshman year with a hope to succeed in show business. In 1940, Muzyad changed his name to Danny Thomas after his youngest and oldest brothers.

Danny married Rose Marie Cassaniti. While a struggling young entertainer with erratic employment, he prayed to Saint Jude Thaddeus, the patron saint of hopeless causes: "Help me find my way in life, and I will build you a shrine." Once at Mass, he put his last seven dollars in the collection basket. The next day he was offered a part that paid ten times the amount he had given to the Church. Danny had experienced the power of prayer. He and Rose were blessed with three children.

Danny was a comedian and a storyteller. "The Danny Thomas Show" ran on CBS radio from 1944–1949. During World War II he entertained the troops and returned to show business after the war. "Make Room for Daddy" appeared on television for eleven years with excellent ratings.

He did not forget that Saint Jude Thaddeus had helped him find his way in life. Danny remembered his promise to Saint Jude. During the 1950s, Danny started raising money to open a children's hospital in Memphis, Tennessee, in honor of Saint Jude. He met with some Memphis businessmen to share his idea of creating a research hospital to treat children with catastrophic diseases.

As a Lebanese Catholic, Danny approached his fellow Americans of Arabic-speaking heritage. Believing deeply that these Americans should thank God for the gift of freedom they enjoy in this country, he invited them to help. In 1957, one hundred representatives of the Arab American community met in Chicago to form the American Lebanese Syrian Associated Charities (ALSAC) with the sole purpose of raising funds for the support of Saint Jude Children's Research Hospital. Today, ALSAC raises five hundred million dollars annually to support the hospital that treats children with leukemia and other cancers.

Saint Jude Children's Hospital opened and was dedicated in 1962. It now has daily operating expenses of two million dollars per day. Saint Jude's physicians and scientists have pioneered treatments that have increased survival rates for childhood cancers from twenty percent when the hospital opened to eighty percent today.

Danny Thomas prayed to God. He asked Saint Jude to help him to find his way in life. In the middle of a successful career in show business, Danny Thomas remembered to show his gratitude to God. Danny Thomas said "thank you" to God in a profoundly moving and fruitful way that continues to bless others.

1. Define the word "temptation."

2. What can you learn about temptation and sin from these passages?

Luke 17:1–2
1 Corinthians 8:12
1 Corinthians 10:13
James 1:13–15
CCC 538
CCC 2287

* Share some effective means you have learned to overcome temptation in your life.

3. How often can God forgive someone who falls into temptation and sins?

Luke 17:3–4
CCC 2845

** Are you a forgiving person, or do you hold onto un-forgiveness or bitterness?

4. Define the word "faith." CCC 26

5. What can you learn about faith from these verses?

Luke 17:5–6
1 Timothy 1:18–19
Hebrews 11:1ff
CCC 154–155
CCC 162

* List some faith-filled people you know. Who would you ask to pray in crisis?

6. Compare the following passages.

Luke 12:37
Luke 17:7–10
John 13:3–5

7. What is our duty toward God?

Luke 17:10
CCC 2087
CCC 2088

8. What can you recall about Samaritans?

John 4:9
Luke 9:51
Luke 10:33–37
Luke 17:11

9. Explain the drama of Jesus cleansing the lepers.

Luke 17:11–13
Luke 17:14
Luke 17:15–16
Luke 17:17–19

10. What posture did the leper choose; what facilitated his healing? Luke 17:16, 19

11. Define the words "thanksgiving" and "gratitude."

12. What can you learn about thanksgiving to God?

Psalm 92:1
Luke 17:16–17
CCC 224
CCC 1333
CCC 2781

* How and when do you praise and thank God?

13. What do the Pharisees want to know? Luke 17:20–21

14. Describe the Son of man when He comes again. Luke 17:24; Daniel 7:13

15. What does Jesus foretell once again? Luke 9:22; 17:25

16. What were people doing in the days of Noah and the Flood? Luke 17:26–27

17. What should one do at the Second Coming? Luke 17:31

18. Explain the conundrum posed by Jesus in Luke 17:33.

19. What interesting aspect can you find about God's divine selection?

Luke 17:34
Luke 17:35

20. Explain Luke 17:37 in your own words. (1 Thessalonians 5:1–2 will help).

*Make a list of people you should thank. In spoken word or in a letter, do so.

CHAPTER 17

Entry into Jerusalem
Luke 18–19

*As he was now drawing near, at the descent of the Mount of Olives,
the whole multitude of the disciples
began to rejoice and praise God with a loud voice
for all the mighty works that they had seen, saying,
"Blessed is the King who comes in the name of the Lord!
Peace in heaven and glory in the highest!"*
Luke 19:37–38

Prayer—Jesus explains to the disciples that He must suffer, die, and rise again, and then He will leave them. While they wait for His return in glory, and while they are suffering, they must always *pray and not lose heart* (Luke 18:1). When Jesus returns, will He find faith? Three parables reveal three aspects of prayer: humility, perseverance, and trust. The widow represents the oppressed and defenseless, suffering at the hands of the ruthless and unjust. God, who is just and merciful, contrasts with the unjust judge.

> God is not accustomed to refusing a good gift to those who ask for one. Since He is good, and especially to those who are faithful to Him, let us hold fast to Him with all our soul, our heart, our strength, and so enjoy His light and see His glory and possess the grace of supernatural joy. Let us reach out with our hearts to possess that good, let us exist in it and live in it, let us hold fast to it, that good which is beyond all we can know or see and is marked by perpetual peace and tranquility, a peace which is beyond all we can know or understand.
> Saint Ambrose, Bishop (340–397), *Treatise on Flight from the World*, 6, 36

The parable of the self-righteous Pharisee and the repentant tax collector illustrates the virtue of humility in prayer. The Pharisee does not seek God's justification, since he already justifies himself. He fasts twice a week, probably on market days, when all can witness his superficial piety. Whereas the tax collector, standing afar, does not even lift his eyes to heaven, but *beat his breast, saying, "God, be merciful to me a sinner!"* (Luke 18:13). For hundreds of years prior to the Second Vatican Council, during the Penitential Rite of the Mass, people would strike their breast three times and pray "through my fault, through my fault, through my most grievous fault." Thankfully, these words and this practice have been restored to the liturgy.

The theme of humility continues as people bring infants to Jesus. Here, Luke uses the Greek word *breph* for "babies," instead of *paidia* for "children." Infants and babes can do nothing for themselves. They are totally dependent upon adults for their nourishment and care. The disciples of Jesus must remain totally dependent upon God and trust during the difficult times to come. The kingdom of God belongs to the humble, prayerful, perseverant, innocent, and trusting souls.

A rich, young ruler, perhaps a synagogue leader, receives a powerful invitation from Jesus: *Sell all that you have and distribute to the poor, and you will have treasure in heaven; and come, follow me* (Luke 18:22). He cannot accept Jesus' invitation because of his attachment to his considerable wealth. Some people have had the grace to accept the invitation of God to give up everything to follow Him. Peter exclaims, *Behold, <u>we</u> have left our homes and followed you* (Luke 18:28). Peter left his home and thriving business to follow Jesus, who acknowledges his sacrifice with an assurance: *Truly, I say to you, there is no man who has left house or wife or brothers or parents or children, for the sake of the kingdom of God, who will not receive manifold more in this time, and in the age to come eternal life* (Luke 18:29–30). Missionaries, from the time of Jesus until now, leave behind everything and pour out their lives in order to spread the Gospel.

Jesus predicts suffering again—Previously, in Luke 9:22; 13:31–33; and 17:25, Jesus foretold His Passion and death in Jerusalem. Now, He clearly tells the Twelve: *Behold, we are going up to Jerusalem, and everything that is written of the Son of man by the prophets will be accomplished. For he will be delivered to the Gentiles [Herod and Pilate], and will be mocked and shamefully treated and spit upon; they will scourge him and kill him, and on the third day he will rise* (Luke 18:31–33). The Apostles cannot understand this yet. The crucifixion will fulfill the promise of God for a Savior to redeem the world. Jesus is the Suffering Servant (Psalms 22; 69; Isaiah 53) who will restore the broken relationship between God and humanity.

In contrast to the Apostles, who *cannot see* or understand what Jesus tries to tell them, the blind man near Jericho "sees" and understands who Jesus is—*Jesus, Son of David, have mercy on me!* (Luke 18:38). Twice before, Luke reported that Jesus gave sight to the blind (4:18; 7:22). Twice before, Jesus told His disciples to invite the blind to their tables (14:32, 21). Now, a blind man, with the eyes of faith, identifies Jesus with the messianic title, *Son of David*. The blind man near Jericho has a vibrant, active faith. He shouts out. He persists, despite his neighbors ordering him to be quiet. He perseveres in prayer. Jesus hears and heals him. The man follows Jesus, glorifies God, and all the people give praise to God.

A rich man finds salvation—When Jesus enters Jericho, one of the oldest, continuously inhabited cities in the world dating back ten thousand years, He meets a very rich, chief tax collector. Jericho, called the City of Palms, was the Palm Springs, California of its day. With its warm climate, Jericho became the perfect place for the rich and famous to recreate. Herod the Great built a palace there for his winter residence. In this city Jesus meet Zacchaeus. Although Zacchaeus was rich, he was also small of stature. So, he climbed a tree to see Jesus. Children especially love to recount this Bible event. Some people will overcome any obstacle to meet the Lord.

Jesus invites Himself to dine at Zacchaeus' home and is received joyfully. But others murmur because Jesus chooses to be the guest of a sinner. The name *Zacchaeus* means "clean" or "pure one." Jesus crosses the lines between clean, righteous Jews and unclean sinners. Zacchaeus does all that is needed for salvation. He seeks out Jesus and dines with Him. He repents of his sins and promises to make restitution and give alms to the poor. He obeys Jesus. Due to his perseverance, Jesus says: *Today salvation has come to this house, since he also is a son of Abraham. For the Son of man came to seek and to save the lost* (Luke 19:9–10). Behold, a wealthy man in the Palm City finds salvation. Jesus loves both the rich and the poor.

In the parable of the ten pounds (a pound equals three months' wages), the emphasis falls not so much on the industry of the servants, although those who are industrious are praised, as on the *nobleman* who became *king*. The citizens hate the king and do not want him to rule over them. This rejection of the king was previously foretold when Jesus described His Passion and death (Luke 18:31–34). Luke contrasts the positive acceptance of Jesus by the common people, with the rejection of Jesus the King by the religious leaders. This last of the three Lucan servant parables shows that servants, who are faithful to Jesus, will be rewarded richly and given even greater responsibility, whereas, those people who reject God's rule and become enemies of Jesus will experience eternal death.

Jerusalem—Jesus makes His triumphal entry into the city of David on a colt, on which no one had ridden, in fulfillment of the prophecy: *Rejoice greatly, O daughter of Zion! Shout aloud, O daughter of Jerusalem! Behold, your king comes to you; triumphant and victorious is he, humble and riding on a donkey, on a colt the foal of a donkey* (Zechariah 9:9). Jews familiar with this prophecy would recognize a king coming in peace. A warrior king would ride a horse. Unlike the palm branches mentioned in other Gospels, Luke mentions that people offered their cloaks, their most precious and costly garments, to spread on the road before Jesus.

One pilgrimage psalm proclaims: *Blessed be he who enters in the name of the LORD! We bless you from the house of the LORD. The LORD is God, and he has given us light. Bind the festal procession with branches, up to the horns of the altar! You are my God, and I will give thanks to you; you are my God, I will extol you* (Psalm 118:26–28). Jesus the King makes His triumphal entry into the holy city and proceeds to the temple. The people rejoice and proclaim the mighty works Jesus has done. *Blessed is the King who comes in the name of the Lord! Peace in heaven and glory in the highest!* (Luke 19:38). Recall the angelic pronouncement to the shepherds in Bethlehem at Jesus' birth: *Glory to God in the highest, and on earth peace among men with whom he is pleased!* (Luke 2:14).

Jesus' whole mission on earth is to bring heaven's gift of peace to sinful men and women, and to reconcile the broken relationship between the all-holy God and fallen humanity. The Pharisees clearly understand the implication and implore Jesus to silence His disciples. Jesus recalls Habakkuk, *for the stone will cry out from the wall* (Habakkuk 2:11). The believers feel compelled to praise the King of kings.

Jesus loved Jerusalem. As a boy, He went to the temple in Jerusalem with Joseph and Mary (Luke 2:41–42) for the feast of Passover. He would have sung pilgrimage psalms on the way. *I was glad [rejoiced] when they said to me, "Let us go to the house of the LORD!" Our feet have been standing within your gates, O Jerusalem!* (Psalm 122:1–2). Jesus would have recalled the words of the prophet Isaiah: *But be glad and rejoice for ever in that which I create; for behold, I create Jerusalem a rejoicing, and her people a joy* (Isaiah 65:18).

Now, Jesus weeps over Jerusalem. His lament has a prophetic tone. Jeremiah, Isaiah, and Hosea all felt the frustration, anger, and sorrow of God for Israel. The city, whose name means "peace," refuses to embrace the Prince of Peace. Jesus issues a prophetic utterance of impending doom. *For the days shall come upon you, when your enemies will cast up a bank about you and surround you, and hem you in on every side, and dash you to the ground, you and your children within you, and they will not leave one stone upon another in you; because you did not know the time of your visitation* (Luke 19:43–44). This terrible prophesy comes true in AD 70 when a Roman army led by Titus, with Tiberius Julius Alexander as second in command, besieges the city. The historian Josephus reports that 1.1 million inhabitants were killed, mostly Jews, and another ninety-seven thousand were captured and enslaved. Titus destroyed the second temple and abolished the high priesthood. *For these things I weep; my eyes flow with tears; for a comforter is far from me, one to revive my courage; my children are desolate, for the enemy has prevailed* (Lamentation 1:16). The heart of Jesus grieves over the horrors to come to His beloved city.

Jesus cleanses the temple—The Temple enters the temple. Jesus began His ministry teaching in the temple (Luke 2:41–51) and ends His ministry teaching in the temple (Luke 20:1–21:38). The temple exists for worshiping God, instructing the people concerning God's law and commandments, and sacrificing to God. Ultimately, it is God's dwelling place. Traders and moneychangers conduct business in the temple. They fleece the poor and do not contribute to divine worship. These traders love the riches of God more than God. Even the priests allow these abuses, perhaps because they receive financial remuneration from them. These materialistic enterprises conflict with spiritual practices. Jesus recalls the words of the prophet Jeremiah: *Has this house, which is called by my name, become a den of robbers in your eyes? Behold, I myself have seen it, says the LORD* (Jeremiah 7:11). With righteous anger, Jesus drives out the traders from the temple.

Today, Jesus dwells in the Eucharist in the tabernacle in every Catholic church and chapel in the world. Jesus' behavior demonstrates how much respect the house of the Lord deserves. Perhaps there are ways in which faithful believers could enhance the reverence shown to Our Lord in His house when coming to worship.

Jesus taught in the temple every day. The chief priests and scribes sought to destroy Him. Jesus challenged the status quo. Some Pharisees did not want change. The example of the Pharisee and the publican shows how prayer and an examination of conscience can help determine whether one is pleasing to God and on the right path.

A Humble Woman of Prayer

All she ever wanted was to be a good wife and mother. She never made a lot of money, never went to college, and never wore designer clothes. She was a happy, faith-filled homemaker in the Midwest. While pregnant with her fourth child, her husband collapsed with a fatal heart attack. She buried her husband on what would have been her tenth wedding anniversary.

Later, she delivered a son and named him after Saint Anthony. She loved her children, worked, played, and laughed. But mostly she prayed. Her oldest son won a full athletic scholarship to college. Before his first game, she asked the coach how her son would be able to go to Mass before the game. "I beg your pardon," the coach exclaimed. She replied, "How will he get to Mass? You keep the players in a hotel so they don't go out and drink and get rowdy. My son isn't like that. But he does go to daily Mass." The coach gawked as mother and son went to Mass.

Later, Tony entered high school and confided that he was not athletically gifted, like his older brother. "That's okay, Tony. God did not make you to be like anyone else. God made you to be you. What do you want to be?" Tony wanted to be an accountant, but was having difficulty in his accounting class. She replied, "Okay, Tony, your mother will help you." Tony was surprised. "You understand accounting, Mom?" "No," she replied, "I don't understand accounting. But you will go and study hard, and I will go and pray hard." Later that week Tony came home exuberant. He had earned the highest grade in the class!

When her oldest son married and he and his wife were joyfully expecting their first baby, the doctor announced that a prenatal exam had detected a birth defect. He advised them to terminate the pregnancy. "This is my child. I am the father. I would never destroy my child." He stayed strong until he got his wife home. Then, he drove to his mother's house and broke down. "Mom, what will we do?" he cried. "Don't worry," she said. "God is good. He has a plan. We will pray and wait, and see what God does." A few months later, a beautiful baby was born, perfect in every way, except for one tiny toe that needed to be separated from the next one.

Everyone who met her marveled at her deep faith. If someone needed prayer, she would be on speed dial, because it seemed that she had an open and direct line to the Almighty. She had not been given an easy life. But, she loved God. She prayed with humility and trust. She persevered in prayer. Her picture never appeared on the cover of a magazine. She never received any awards. But she blessed all of the people whose lives she touched, who came to know her and love her.

"Spread love everywhere you go . . . let no one ever come to you without leaving happier. Be the living expression of God's kindness."
Blessed Mother Teresa

1. Explain the parable in Luke 18:1–8.

2. What virtue does the widow demonstrate?

Ephesians 6:18
Hebrews 12:1
CCC 2728
CCC 2742

3. Describe the self-appraisal of the Pharisee below.

Luke 18:10–11
Luke 18:12

4. Contrast this with the prayer of the tax collector.

Luke 18:13
CCC 2631

5. How does Saint Peter affirm Luke 18:14? 1 Peter 5:6

6. Describe the drama in Luke 18:15–17.

7. What does it mean to *receive the kingdom of God like a child*? Luke 18:17

8. Outline the exchange between Jesus and the rich ruler.

Luke 18:18
Luke 18:19–20
Luke 18:21
Luke 18:22
Luke 18:23

9. What truths can your glean from these verses?

Luke 18:24–25
Luke 18:26–27
Luke 18:28
Luke 18:29–30

10. What does Jesus foretell for the third time? Luke 18:31–34

11. Describe the exchange between the blind man and Jesus.

Luke 18:35–39
Luke 18:40–41
Luke 18:42

12. What happened after the blind man received his sight? Luke 18:43

13. Explain the meeting between Jesus and Zacchaeus.

Luke 19:1–4
Luke 19:5
Luke 19:8
Luke 19:9

14. Why did Jesus come to earth? Luke 19:10

15. Find the most significant aspect of the parable of the pounds. Luke 19:47, 27

16. Describe Jesus' triumphal entry into Jerusalem.

Zechariah 9:9
Luke 19:28–33
Luke 19:35–36
2 Kings 9:13
Luke 19:37
Luke 19:38
CCC 559
CCC 560

17. Describe the exchange between the Pharisees and Jesus.

Luke 19:39
Luke 19:40
Habakkuk 2:11

18. What can you learn from the following verses?

Luke 19:41
Luke 19:42
Luke 19:43–44
Isaiah 29:1–3 *(Ariel–poetic name for Jerusalem)*
Jeremiah 6:6
Ezekiel 4:1–3
1 Peter 2:12

19. Why did Jesus cleanse the temple? Luke 19:45–46

20. What was the people's response to Jesus' teaching in the temple? Luke 19:47–48

* List three ways to show more respect in God's house today.

Chapter 18

Watchfulness
Luke 20–21

And there will be signs in sun and moon and stars,
and upon the earth distress of nations
in perplexity at the roaring of the sea and the waves,
men fainting with fear and with foreboding at what is coming on the world;
for the powers of the heavens will be shaken.
And then they will see the Son of man coming in a cloud
with power and great glory.
Now when these things begin to take place, look up and raise your heads,
because your redemption is drawing near.
Luke 21:25–28

The Journey to Jerusalem, which Jesus began in Luke 9:51, ends now in the temple where Jesus will proclaim the will of God to the people. From now until His death, Jesus will stay in and around Jerusalem. As Jesus speaks to the people, the chief priests, scribes, and elders challenge His authority to teach in the temple. Jesus skillfully turns the table on them and asks them the origin of John's baptism. They are trapped and they know it. So, they refuse to answer, and Jesus does the same.

The parable of the wicked tenants (Luke 20:9–18) uses common Old Testament imagery to identify the source of Jesus' authority to teach—Jesus is the Beloved Son of God. Jesus gives a final warning to the leaders about the terrible consequences of rejecting the Messiah and announces that He knows that He will be crucified. The characters in the parable follow the Old Testament parable in Isaiah 5:1–7.

> Vineyard = Israel
> Tenants = Religious Leaders
> Servants = Prophets
> Vineyard Owner = God
> Beloved Son = Jesus

Jesus knows and proclaims that He is the stone rejected by the leaders, which becomes the cornerstone of the Church—God's new structure. Peter later explains, *To you therefore who believe, he is precious, but for those who do not believe, "The very stone which the builders rejected has become the cornerstone," and "A stone that will make men stumble, a rock that will make them fall"* (1 Peter 2:7–8).

Undaunted, the leaders come with false flattery and set a seemingly perfect trap for Jesus. They ask about paying taxes. They expect that Jesus will either disappoint the common people or appear as a tax evader to the Romans. Jesus' response is simple, profound, and ingenious. *Render to Caesar the things that are Caesar's, and to God the things that are God's* (Luke 20:25). People rightly identify the importance of maintaining the proper relationship between church and state. However, Jesus teaches an even deeper, more profound truth. A human being is a child of God, made in the image and likeness of God. Contemporary society wrongly assumes personal ownership of one's body, but Jesus proclaims the truth. Paul reiterates: *Do you not know that your body is a temple of the Holy Spirit within you, which you have from God? You are not your own; you were bought with a price. So glorify God in your body* (1 Corinthians 6:19–20).

For the first time in Luke's Gospel, Sadducees appear. Sadducees, a priestly party descending from Zadok the priest (1 Kings 1:8), believed only in the Pentateuch. Sadducees denied the existence of angels, the resurrection of the body, with its rewards and punishments, and the existence of the immortal soul. They present Jesus with an absurd question concerning a concept that they do not even believe. One primary blessing of marriage is children. Progeny allow for the inheritance of the family land. In ancient Israel, a Levirate law required a man to marry the childless widow of his brother, in order to provide heirs for his brother and keep his land in the family. In heaven, there is no longer marriage, childbearing, or death. Jesus skillfully uses a Scripture that the Sadducees accept to prove the point. *I am the God of your father, the God of Abraham, the God of Isaac, and the God of Jacob* (Exodus 3:6). God is the friend of Abraham. While people die, God does not. He is eternal. God's relationship with the patriarchs is everlasting. Hence, logically, if God *is* the God of Abraham, Abraham must still exist.

Jesus turns the tables on the questioners again, and asks about the relationship between King David and the Messiah. The actual Davidic dynasty ended in 586 BC. Jesus proves that He is both the son of David (Luke 1:27; Matthew 1:20) and David's Lord, to whom David prayed: *The LORD says to my lord* (Psalm 110:1).

Since they are going to say that the Christ is the son of David, David himself prophesies, fearing and understanding the error of sinners: "The Lord said to my Lord, sit at my right hand, until I make of your enemies a footstool to your feet." And again Isaiah says as follows: "The Lord said to Christ my Lord, whose right hand I upheld, that the nations should obey Him—and I will shatter the strength of kings." See how David calls Him *Lord* and does not say *son*.

Letter of Barnabas (AD 70), 12, 9

The widow's mite—Jesus denounces the hypocrisy of the scribes, who wear long robes. Because scribes could read and write documents, they wrote and executed wills. Therefore, widows and orphans, who usually could not read, were at the mercy of the scribes. The scribe would determine his fee for reading the will and assign a sum of money for the heirs to give to the temple. In contrast to the showy and unscrupulous behavior of the scribes, Jesus praises a poor widow, who gives two small coins, worth less than a penny, out of her want and poverty.

Warnings—Jesus warns about critical events to come: the destruction of Jerusalem and the temple, the persecution of believers, the end of the world, and the Second Coming of Christ. These warnings are as important today as they were in the first century. Every believer must repent, believe in Jesus, and remain in a state of grace, for no one knows the time of judgment.

Solomon's temple was destroyed in 586 BC, and a simpler temple was built after the Babylonian captivity ended. Herod the Great, who admired great architecture, drew up plans to rebuild the temple in 20 BC. Herod Agrippa II completed the final touches on the temple in AD 64. Much of the renovated structure was completed when Jesus spoke, and the temple provided a resplendent sight for pilgrims to the city. But Jesus rightly predicts that the magnificent edifice will be destroyed. Common people are amazed and afraid. Jesus gives the people three exhortations.

---

1) Do not be led astray (Luke 21:8)
2) Do not fear (Luke 21:9)
3) Be watchful and pray (Luke 21:36)

Christians will be persecuted in the early Church and throughout history. Jesus suffered and disciples also suffer. Jesus warns the disciples of persecutions to come and tells them to persevere; a reward will come in eternity for those who suffer well. Paul tells his disciple Timothy: *Indeed all who desire to live a godly life in Christ Jesus will be persecuted* (2 Timothy 3:12). Even family members will hate and betray their brethren. Martyrs for Christ stand firm in every age. *By your endurance you will gain your lives* (Luke 21:19). Peter warns believers to be watchful and stand strong against the evil one: *Be sober, be watchful. Your adversary the devil prowls around like a roaring lion, seeking some one to devour. Resist him, firm in your faith, knowing that the same experience of suffering is required of your brotherhood throughout the world* (1 Peter 5:8–9).

The early Christians remembered the warnings of Jesus, even forty years later. Jesus' predictions of the signs of impending disaster were so clear and specific that when the Christians living in Jerusalem in AD 70 saw the Roman armies led by Titus coming, and the signs Jesus had revealed, they fled the city to the Transjordan area. Even though Eusebius reports that 1.1 million people were killed in the siege of Jerusalem, and thousands more captured and enslaved, almost all Jewish Christians were spared. Just as Jesus foretold, the spectacular structure of the temple was completely razed in AD 70, when some of those who had heard Jesus' prediction would have still been alive. Jesus wept over the city of Jerusalem (Luke 19:41–44). Jesus foretold the destruction of the temple and the city of Jerusalem, and some of the believers listened and heeded His warnings.

The Second Coming—Jesus came to earth the first time as a human baby, born of a woman in Bethlehem, in poverty and simplicity (Luke 2:4–7). Jesus tells listeners that He will come again at the end of time in glory, to judge the living and the dead. This event is called Christ's *Parousia*. Jesus judges each person at the moment of death, the "particular judgment." Each individual will enter the blessedness of heaven—either immediately or after a time of purification in purgatory—or be thrust into immediate and everlasting punishment in hell (CCC 1022). When Christ comes again in glory to judge the living and the dead, those who have already died will receive a confirmation of their earlier particular judgment in what is called the "Last Judgment." At the time of the final judgment, all people will see the divine mercy and justice meted out to each person.

So, the coming of the Son of man in glory presents an event of unimaginable joy for faithful believers, but a terror of impending doom for evildoers and those who have refused to accept the mercy offered by God. Paul says: *For the Lord himself will descend from heaven with a cry of command, with the archangel's call, and with the sound of the trumpet of God. And the dead in Christ will rise first; then we who are alive, who are left, shall be caught up together with them in the clouds to meet the Lord in the air; and so we shall always be with the Lord. Therefore comfort one another with these words* (1 Thessalonians 4:16–18). Will you have fear or joyful expectation?

The kingdom of God, which began on earth with the life of Jesus and the establishment of His Church, is not of this world. Jesus will come again to destroy Satan and all his works, and deliver the kingdom of God into the New Jerusalem. The signs of the Second Coming indicate the final consummation of the redemption won by Christ on the Cross. The destruction of Jerusalem symbolizes the end of this world. Jesus assures believers of the veracity of His word. *Heaven and earth will pass away, but my words will not pass away* (Luke 21:33). All of these things will happen exactly as Jesus promised.

Jesus ends His teaching in the temple by encouraging watchfulness and prayer. Some decide to eat, drink, and be merry, and repent at a later time. But no one knows the day or the hour in which this life will come to an end. And suddenly, the end will come to each person, and the end will ultimately come to the entire world. One day, each person must give an accounting of his or her life. The believer practices detachment from the things of this world and strives to draw close to God. Christian virtues and charitable deeds follow into everlasting life.

But watch at all times, praying that you may have strength to escape all these things that will take place, and to stand before the Son of man (Luke 21:36). Jesus gives specific warnings and clear directions. The Second Coming will affect the whole world and determine the fate of each human person. The stakes are very high. So, Jesus warns: (1) do not be led astray, (2) do not fear, but (3) watch and pray. Prayer and the sacraments enable the Catholic to remain in the state of grace and grow in virtue. Frequent celebration of the Sacraments of Reconciliation and Holy Eucharist provide excellent opportunities to stay watchful and ready.

Jesus concludes His teaching in the temple. Even though the leaders want to get rid of Jesus, they do not arrest Him in the temple because the people love Jesus and want to listen to Him. Jesus disrupts the status quo for the chief priests, scribes, and elders. Who does He think He is teaching in their temple? Who taught Him? What are His credentials? By whose authority does He teach? They try to embarrass Him or trap Him in front of His attentive listeners, but they fail. They want to arrest Jesus, but He outwits them. They fail to see the kingdom of God unfolding before their very eyes. Their hearts are hardened. And now, dark clouds gather.

The Day of the Lord

Oh, what a day that will be, and how great when it comes, dearest brethren! when the Lord begins to survey His people and to recognize by examining with divine knowledge the merits of each individual! to cast into hell evildoers, and to condemn our persecutors to the eternal fire and punishing flame! and indeed, to present to us the reward of faith and devotion! What will be that glory, and how great the joy of being admitted to the sight of God! to be so honored as to receive the joy of eternal light and salvation in the presence of Christ the Lord, your God! to greet Abraham, and Isaac, and Jacob, and all the patriarchs, apostles, prophets, and martyrs! to rejoice with the just and with the friends of God in the kingdom of heaven, in the delight of the immortality that will be given! to receive there what eye has not seen nor ear heard, what has not entered into the heart of man!

The Apostle predicts that we will receive even greater things than we perform or suffer here, when he says: *The sufferings of the present time are not worth comparing with the brightness about to come upon us and which will be unveiled in us* (Romans 8:18). When that unveiling has come and when the brightness of God shines about us, honored by the condescension of the Lord, we shall be as blessed and joyful as they will remain guilty and miserable—those deserters of God and rebels against God, who have done the will of the devil, so that it is necessary for them to be tortured with him in the unquenchable fire.

Saint Cyprian of Carthage (AD 253),
Letter of Cyprian to the People of Thibar,
58 (56), 10

1. Explain the challenge to Jesus' authority. How does Jesus respond? Luke 20:1–8

2. Compare the parables in Isaiah 5:1–7 and Luke 20:9–16.

Isaiah 5:1–7	Luke 20:9–16

3. What can you learn from these verses?

Psalm 118:22–23
Isaiah 8:14–15
Luke 20:17–18
Acts 4:10–12

4. How did the scribes try to trip up Jesus on taxes? Luke 20:19–26

5. What part of you belongs to God? Luke 20:25; 1 Corinthians 6:19–20

* How can you glorify God in your body?

6. What puzzle do the Sadducees present to Jesus? Luke 20:27–33

7. What truth does Jesus teach?

Luke 20:34–38
CCC 366
CCC 989–991
CCC 993

8. What is Jesus' relationship to David?

Psalm 110:1
Luke 20:41–44

9. What did Jesus warn the disciples about the scribes? Luke 20:45–47

** Who or what do you think Jesus would warn people about today?

10. Why does Jesus compliment the poor widow? Luke 21:1–4

11. What does Jesus foretell in Luke 21:5–7?

12. Find two warnings and two commands that Jesus gives in Luke 21:8–9.

13. List some signs of the persecution to come.

Luke 21:10–11
Luke 21:12
Luke 21:13–17

14. How should a believer prepare for times of persecution? Luke 21:13–14

* Prepare and share the Gospel and your testimony in five minutes for your group.

15. What does Jesus foretell in Luke 21:20–24?

16. What are some signs of the Second Coming of Jesus? Luke 21:25–26

17. Describe what people will see? Luke 21:27

18. If you are alive at that time, what should you do? Luke 21:28

19. What should believers do until the Lord comes again? Luke 21:34–36

20. How does Saint Paul encourage the early Christians? 1 Thessalonians 5:6–11

* List some practical things to do to prepare for the coming of the Lord.

Monthly Social Activity

This month, your small group will meet for coffee, tea, or a simple breakfast, lunch, or dessert in someone's home. Pray for this social event and for the host or hostess. Try, if at all possible, to attend.

Share a way in which you might prepare for judgment.

Some examples:

 — *Just keep on doing what I'm doing.*

 — *Examine my conscience every night.*

 — *Get to Confession once a month.*

 — *Try to heal a broken relationship,
    before it's too late.*

CHAPTER 19

Last Supper
Luke 22

This is my body which is given for you.
Do this in remembrance of me.
Luke 22:19

The devil tempted Jesus in the wilderness *and when the devil had ended every temptation, he departed from him until an opportune time* (Luke 4:13) would come. Well, the opportune time has now come. As the chief priests and scribes were looking for a way to put Jesus to death, *Satan entered into Judas called Iscariot* (Luke 22:3). All four Gospels identify Judas as the betrayer, but John also calls him a *thief* (John 12:6). First, the devil suggests that he can pilfer from the poor box, and then, after many small betrayals, Satan leads him to seek silver by selling the Teacher Himself. Judas illustrates what has been called "the banality of evil." Perhaps at one time he had expected Jesus to be a warrior king who would provide plenty of booty. Whatever his original intentions, Judas eventually comes down on the wrong side of the cosmic battle between good and evil.

Jesus celebrates a final meal with His disciples. Matthew, Mark, and Luke place this on the eve of Passover; John puts the meal a night earlier. This discrepancy can be addressed by recognizing the slightly different Jewish calendars then in use. On the first Passover, halfway through the lunar month of Nissan (March/April), God caused the angel of death to pass over the homes of the Hebrews and allowed them to escape from slavery in Egypt (Exodus 12–13). God ordained that all Jews should gather annually at that time of year for a meal of remembrance. The Torah required three menu items: (1) bitter herbs, to remind them of the bitter taste of slavery; 2) unleavened bread, because they left so fast that there was no time for bread to rise; and 3) a one-year-old unblemished male lamb, whose blood on their lintels caused the angel of death to pass over.

Jesus sent Peter and John to find a man carrying a water jug, whose master would provide them with a room. Usually women toted water, but rich people might send a male servant. Large homes in ancient times had a guest room on the roof, accessible by outdoor stairs. At festival time these rooms were often let out for the use of pilgrim groups who flooded the city. No one offered Joseph, Mary, and soon-to-be-born Jesus any hospitality in the inn, *kataluma* (Luke 2:7), because there was no room. Now, some generous soul gave a Passover welcome to Jesus and His Apostles in a guest room, *kataluma* (Luke 22:11), and Jesus would be the host.

Jesus knows that this night begins His Passover from life to death. On this Last Supper, Jesus does something so extraordinary that the Apostles must have been stunned. Jesus interrupts the traditional Passover ritual with words that are radically shocking and transformational. Jesus knows that He will be crucified within twenty-four hours. On this Last Supper, Jesus institutes the priesthood and the Eucharist, by which He will remain with believers for millennia to come. The Last Supper offers the sacrifice of Calvary prior to the event, through Jesus' power and His words of consecration. The sacrifice prefigured by Abel (Genesis 4:4), Abraham (Genesis 15:9–10), and Melchizedek (Genesis 14:18–20) now reaches perfection in the supreme sacrifice of Christ, which replaces the old sacrificial system.

Four institution narratives record the Last Supper and Jesus bestowing the gift of the Eucharist (Matthew 26:26–29; Mark 14:22–25; Luke 22:15–20; 1 Corinthians 11:23–26). Luke's is the longest of these narratives. It closely resembles that of Paul, since they shared the Eucharist many times over at least a decade of travels (AD 50–60). By combining material from the two sources, one can partially reconstruct the Anaphora, or Eucharistic Prayer, used by the Pauline communities.

LUCAN/PAULINE ANAPHORA

Preface from Luke

And when the hour came, he sat at table, and the apostles with him. And he said to them, "I have earnestly desired to eat this Passover with you before I suffer; for I tell you I shall not eat it until it is fulfilled in the kingdom of God." And he took a chalice, and when he had given thanks he said, "Take this, and divide it among yourselves; for I tell you that from now on I shall not drink of the fruit of the vine until the kingdom of God comes" (Luke 22:14–18).

Material Shared by Luke and Paul

And he took bread, and when he had given thanks he broke it and gave it to them, saying, "This is my body which is given for you. Do this in remembrance of me." And likewise the chalice after supper, saying, "This chalice which is poured out for you is the new covenant in my blood" (Luke 22:19–20; cf. 1 Corinthians 11:23–25).

Epilogue from Paul

"Do this, as often as you drink it, in remembrance of me." For as often as you eat this bread and drink the chalice, you proclaim the Lord's death until he comes. Whoever, therefore, eats the bread or drinks the cup of the Lord in an unworthy manner will be guilty of profaning the body and blood of the Lord (1 Corinthians 11:26–27).

Luke has two cups, a Cup of Blessing and a Cup of Eucharist, while Paul has only the second of these. This difference arises only because they are quoting different sections of the same source. Paul has two memorial imperatives, *Do this* (1 Corinthians 11:24–25), one after the consecration of the bread and the other after the consecration of the cup. Luke has only the first of these, which seems a bit awkward standing between the consecrations. Can the demonstrative "this" point both backwards and forwards? Again, this apparent difference has arisen only because the edit points were different. The Mozarabic Rite of ancient Spain retained the Pauline double imperative; the Roman Rite has always had just a single memorial imperative, following the second consecration.

In Lucan language, the Eucharist is referred to as the *breaking of the bread* (Luke 24:35). The very first Christian community in Jerusalem continued to worship at the temple but celebrated the *breaking [of the] bread in their homes* (Acts 2:46). The breaking of the Sacred Host, called "Fraction" in the Roman Rite, is one of the most solemn moments of the Mass, so much so that the liturgy would be incomplete without it. This sacred action pertains both to the Last Supper and to Calvary.

In the second century, a powerful testament to the reality of Christ's self-giving sacrifice comes from Saint Justin the Martyr:

> We call this food *Eucharist;* and no one is permitted to partake of it, except one who believes our teaching to be true, and who has been washed in the washing, which is for the remission of sins and for regeneration, and is thereby living as Christ has enjoined. For not as common bread, nor common drink, do we receive these; but since Jesus Christ our Savior was made incarnate by the word of God and had both flesh and blood for our salvation, so too, as we have been taught, the food which has been made into the Eucharist by the Eucharistic prayer set down by Him, and by the change of which our blood and flesh is nourished, is both the flesh and the blood of that incarnated Jesus.
>
> Saint Justin the Martyr (AD 100–165), *First Apology,* 66

Two centuries later, Saint Ambrose, Bishop of Milan, explains the real change that takes place during the celebration of the liturgy:

> Before it be consecrated it is bread; but where the words of Christ come in, it is the Body of Christ. Finally, hear Him saying: "All of you take and eat of this; for this is My Body." And before the words of Christ the chalice is full of wine and water, but where the words have been operative it is made the Blood of Christ, which redeems people.
>
> Saint Ambrose of Milan (AD 333–339), *The Sacraments,* 4, 5, 23

Transubstantiation—All Catholic bishops met in the Fourth Lateran Council in Rome in 1215. Among the doctrines promulgated was "transubstantiation"; the substances of bread and wine, while retaining their appearances, are totally transformed into the Eucharistic Body, Blood, Soul, and Divinity of Christ. The same man born of Mary, circumcised in the flesh, scourged and beaten, crucified and now risen is given whole and entire to the worthy recipient of Holy Communion. Fifty years later, Saint Thomas Aquinas teaches that in the Eucharist four of our five senses are deceived, and so we must rely on hearing alone. The voice that spoke the words, *This is my Body* (Luke 22:19) is the same voice that had said, *Let there be light* (Genesis 1:3). Everything is what God says it is, and by that same authority Jesus recreates the essences of bread and wine into Himself.

The Second Vatican Council affirmed that the faithful have an obligation as well as a right to participate as fully as possible in the Holy Sacrifice of the Mass. As Jesus is truly present to us in the Eucharist, we should be truly present to Him. The command *Do this* (Luke 22:19) is not just an invitation to receive, but also to join in giving. Every day, four hundred thousand priests and bishops throughout the world repeat these words of Christ, and also repeat His actions. The faithful people who physically attend these earthly liturgies become spiritually present at the Divine Liturgy. There is only one sacrifice of the Mass—that offered by Christ. The action is re-presented, but the event is the same. The Last Supper and Calvary are the only events of history at which we can be truly present, by participating in the Mass.

As they left the upper room, Jesus and the disciples could hear thousands of other pilgrims singing the Egyptian Hallel (Psalms 113–118), proper to all the great festivals. Along with them, Judas Iscariot should have sung, *blessed be the name of the* Lord (Psalm 113:2). Along with them, the temple priests should have sung, *Judah became his sanctuary, Israel his dominion* (Psalm 114:2). Along with them, the temple guards should have sung, *The right hand of the* Lord *is exalted; the right hand of the* Lord *does valiantly!* (Psalm 118:16). Impervious to the sound of the singing pilgrims, they sang another song, which was not God's song.

The Agony in the Garden (First Sorrowful Mystery of the Rosary)—Once they reach the garden of the Kidron Valley (John 18:1), also called Gethsemane (Matthew 26:36; Mark 14:32), on the slopes of the Mount of Olives (Luke 22:39), Jesus prays, *Father, if you are willing, remove this chalice from me* (Luke 22:42). The word "chalice" appears three times in this chapter: (1) a pre-Eucharistic chalice, (2) a Eucharistic chalice, and (3) a chalice of suffering (Luke 22:17, 20, 42). As He prayed, Jesus was only a stone's throw away from the disciples James and John, whom He once had asked, *Are you able to drink the chalice that I drink?* (Mark 10:38). This very evening they had drunk of the Eucharistic chalice, and now they may begin to understand that they were also called to drink of the chalice of pain. Would they have been so eager to drink from His chalice if they had known about the suffering to follow?

All four evangelists tell of Jesus in the garden, but only Luke describes His experience as an *agony* (Luke 22:44, reduced to a footnote in some translations because of conflicting manuscript testimony). Greeks used the term *agonia* for wrestling, one of their martial arts. Jacob had wrestled with an angel at Jabbok (Genesis 32:22–32). After the devil tempted Jesus in the desert, angels came to comfort Him. Now another angel comes to comfort Him in the garden (Luke 22:43). Luke the physician, in his usual way, gives a somatic aspect to the spiritual event, saying that Jesus poured sweat like drops of blood. Jesus bled the first time at His circumcision (Luke 2:21); He sheds His Precious Blood again in the garden.

The Arrest—The temple guards seize Jesus and take Him into the house of the high priest. The account here assumes two points of view, one outside the house and the other within. Matthew gives more detail about the threefold denials by Peter outside (Matthew 26:69–75). John was known to the high priest and went inside (John 18:15), so he alone reveals there were actually two interrogations, one by Annas and the other by Caiaphas. The accounts of Mark and John interweave the two scenarios, going back and forth between Peter outside and Jesus inside. Matthew puts the interrogation first and the denial second; Luke tells of the denial first and the interrogation second.

Annas and Caiaphas knew that Jewish law forbade night courts. They wanted to seize the opportunity presented by the defection of Judas, but did not follow proper protocol. The seventy-two members of the Sanhedrin were hardly able to gather at a moment's notice on the evening of a great festival. Witnesses could hardly be called out of their beds to give testimony. The proceedings, as described by all four evangelists, were highly irregular. Jesus had rights before any Jewish tribunal, which were not respected by the competent officials in this case. In the presence of the high priest, false witnesses committed the crime of perjury (Matthew 26:60; Mark 14:56). Roman and Jewish readers alike would have considered that a sacrilege.

Scourging at the Pillar (Second Sorrowful Mystery of the Rosary)—During Greek wrestling matches, the referee held a whip. If either player committed a foul, such as gouging the eyes, then the referee would scourge the player until the offender stopped. Hence, the word "agony" already contains within it the suggestion of scourging. In the account of Luke, the temple guards beat Jesus after arresting Him in the night (Luke 22:63), but in two other Gospels the soldiers scourge Him during the daytime (Mark 14:65; John 19:1). Jesus was probably subjected to various kinds of torture through the night and continuing into the morning. The guards and soldiers were charged with protecting the masses of pilgrims at festival time, but their orders did not call for subjecting those who were innocent to physical abuse. For the first time in His life, Jesus sheds blood at the hands of sinners. The sacrifice has begun.

A Jewish calendar day begins at nightfall and continues until the next sundown. Thus, to all the Jewish participants, the events of Holy Thursday evening took place on the same day as those of Good Friday. The events unfold as an unbroken chain connecting the Eucharist with the Cross. According to Catholic liturgical law, hosts consecrated during the Holy Thursday liturgy are distributed to the faithful during the Good Friday liturgy each year. One Lord, one Supper, one Sacrifice.

The Theology of the Words of Institution

Jesus "broke the bread." The breaking of bread for all is in the first instance a function of the head of the family, who by this action in some sense represents God the Father, who gives us everything, through the earth's bounty, that we need for life. It is also a gesture of hospitality, through which the stranger is given a share in what is one's own; he is welcomed into table fellowship. Breaking and distributing: it is the act of distributing that creates community. This archetypally human gesture of giving, sharing, and uniting acquires an entirely new depth in Jesus' Last Supper through his gift of himself. God's bountiful distribution of gifts takes on a radical quality when the Son communicates and distributes himself in the form of bread.

This gesture of Jesus has thus come to symbolize the whole mystery of the Eucharist: in the Acts of the Apostles and in early Christianity generally, the "breaking of bread" designates the Eucharist. In this sacrament we enjoy the hospitality of God, who gives himself to us in Jesus Christ, crucified and risen. Thus breaking bread and distributing it—the act of attending lovingly to those in need—is an intrinsic dimension of the Eucharist.

"Caritas," care for the other, is not an additional sector of Christianity alongside worship; rather, it is rooted in it and forms part of it. The horizontal and the vertical are inseparably linked in the Eucharist, in the "breaking of the bread." In this dual action of praise/thanksgiving and breaking/distributing that is recounted at the beginning of the institution narrative, the essence of the new worship established by Christ through the Last Supper, Cross, and Resurrection is made manifest: here the old Temple worship is abolished and at the same time brought to its fulfillment.

Pope Benedict XVI, *Jesus of Nazareth, II, Holy Week*
(San Francisco, CA: Ignatius Press, 2011),
130–131.

1. Who betrayed Jesus? What can you learn about him?

Luke 22:1–6
John 12:6

2. What can you learn about Passover?

Luke 22:7–15
Exodus 12:1ff
CCC 1130
CCC 1151
CCC 1339

3. Compare the four Institution Narratives.

Matthew 26:26–29
Mark 14:22–25
Luke 22:17–20
1 Corinthians 11:23–26

* Which two are most similar? **What does receiving the Eucharist mean to you?

4. Describe the sad ending of the Last Supper. Luke 22:21–23

5. How does John provide a theological explanation of this event?

John 6:35	
John 6:51	
John 6:53–54	
John 6:57–58	

6. What does Jesus say about true greatness? Luke 22:24–26

7. What do the disciples have to look forward to in the future? Luke 22:28–30

8. What did Jesus foretell about Peter? What did Jesus do for him? Luke 22:31–34

* Who prays for you that your faith will be strong? For whom do you pray?

9. Explain the scenario below.

Luke 22:39–40
Luke 22:41–42
Luke 22:43
Luke 22:44
Luke 22:45–46

10. What can you learn from these segments?

CCC 2605
CCC 2612
CCC 2824

11. Find a word mentioned twice in Luke 22:40–46 that helps avoid temptation.

12. What evidence shows that Jesus knows everything beforehand? Luke 22:47–48

13. Describe the scenario and miracle in Luke 22:49–51.

14. What does Jesus say to the chief priests and elders? Luke 22:52–53

15. Describe Peter's behavior. Luke 22:54–61

16. What happened after Peter's fall? Luke 22:61–62

17. What does Peter's remorse demonstrate? CCC 1428–1429

* How does Peter's fall and repentance give you hope?

18. What did the chief priests and scribes demand of Jesus? Luke 22:66–67a

19. How does Jesus respond? Luke 22:67b–69

20. What can you learn from Luke 22:70–71?

CHAPTER 20

Way of the Cross
Luke 23

Father, forgive them; for they know not what they do.
Luke 23:34

The most widely recognized, supremely meaningful, and momentous death in all of human history is the crucifixion of Jesus of Nazareth. Religious and secular authorities responsible for sentencing Jesus to death may not, at the time, have realized that they were murdering the Son of God, but they certainly knew that they were condemning an innocent man to an unimaginably painful, humiliating death. Thanks to the four evangelists, more is known about the trials of Jesus than of any other ancient judicial processes, except perhaps for the trial of Socrates.

Jesus is condemned to death: First Station of the Cross (Luke 23:1–25)—Pontius Pilate, the Roman prefect who ruled Judea from AD 26–36, was notoriously cruel and corrupt. He was eventually removed when his evil exceeded all bounds. Pilate's concern was not justice, but keeping the civil peace. Before this court, Jesus had no rights, because He was not a Roman citizen. Pilate could execute Jesus for any or no reason at all. John gives the most detailed account of this trial, which occurred on stone pavement in the courtyard of the Antonia Fortress adjacent to the Temple Mount. All four Gospels portray Pilate as reluctant to condemn Jesus. Matthew notes that Pilate's wife, troubled by a bad dream, advises him not to do anything to *that righteous man* (Matthew 27:19). Three times Pilate declares Jesus innocent: (1) *I find no crime in this man,* (2) *I did not find this man guilty of any of your charges against him,* and (3) *nothing deserving death has been done by him* (Luke 23:4, 14, 15).

Luke is the only source of information that Pilate sent Jesus to Herod Antipas. If Herod had confirmed that Jesus came from royal blood, Pilate might have treated him gingerly. Pilate had been sent to serve kings, not to condemn them. So Jesus, who had the right to rule the Land of Israel, appeared before the usurper Herod, who was not of the House of David and thus had no true claim to the throne. The true King appeared before the false one, who had beheaded His cousin John the Baptist. Jesus does not play into the hand of a superstitious, adulterous murderer. *He was oppressed, and he was afflicted, yet he opened not his mouth* (Isaiah 53:7). Herod questions Jesus at length, *but he made no answer* (Luke 23:9). Jesus refuses even to speak to Herod, so Herod mocks Jesus and sends Him back to Pilate.

Ruthless, Pilate and Herod compromise with evil. Cowardly, they give in to the riotous will of troublemakers. They fulfill the words: *Why do the nations conspire and the peoples plot in vain? The kings of the earth set themselves, and the rulers take counsel together, against the LORD and his anointed* (Psalm 2:1–2). Later, Peter recalls the corroboration of Herod and Pilate. *For truly in this city there were gathered together against your holy servant Jesus, whom you anointed, both Herod and Pontius Pilate, with the Gentiles and the peoples of Israel, to do whatever your hand and your plan had predestined to take place* (Acts 4:27–28). Peter shows that all people, Jews and Gentiles, share in the responsibility for Christ's death.

Pilate tries to distract the crowd with a choice between the teacher Jesus and the murderer *Barabbas*, whose name means "son of the father." Tragically, they choose to condemn the real "Son of the Father." Jesus had said: *All things have been delivered to me by my Father; and no one knows who the Son is except the Father, or who the Father is except the Son* (Luke 10:22). On the Last Day, the judicial roles of Good Friday will be reversed. Jesus will judge; and Pilate and Herod, along with all the other judges of history, will appear before Him to be judged. There, they will receive the justice denied to Jesus and many other innocent victims.

Jesus takes up His Cross: Second Station of the Cross—By mid-morning, Jesus had passed a sleepless night going back-and-forth across the city repeatedly, from the upper room on the west to the Kidron Valley in the east, back to the house of the high priest in the west to the Antonia Fortress in the east, back to Herod's palace in the west to the Antonia Fortress in the east again. Before the way of the Cross even began Jesus had crossed the city six times, mostly in shackles. He was dehydrated and weak from blood loss and sleep deprivation. By no means was Jesus in any physical condition to carry the heavy crossbeam alone.

Simon helps Jesus carry His Cross: Fifth Station of the Cross (Luke 23:26)—Simon of Cyrene earns only a single verse in three of the four Gospels (Matthew 27:32; Mark 15:21; Luke 23:26). Mark gives the most information. He says Simon was coming in from the country, suggesting that he was physically fit. The soldiers would have been looking for the strongest man available for this work. Mark then adds the names of the man's two sons. Always, the eldest appears first in such lists, so the father's legal name is "Simon, father of Alexander." A tomb in Jerusalem has been found belonging to "Alexander, son of Simon," datable to the first century.

Luke includes people from *Egypt and the parts of Libya belonging to Cyrene* (Acts 2:10) among those who receive the Holy Spirit on the first Pentecost. Cyrenaica was a very small province, but Cyreneans had a prominent role in the early Church, going up to Antioch to spread the Gospel (Acts 10:20). A certain Lucius from Cyrene even became a member of the inner circle of Antioch (Acts 13:1). The Cyreneans probably were held in high esteem because one of them had helped to lighten the load of the Suffering Servant. Earlier, Jesus had said to all, *If any man would come after me, let him deny himself and take up his cross daily and follow me* (Luke 9:23). Just as Simon takes up the Cross of Christ, each believer is invited to join his or her suffering with Christ's Passion. Suffering comes to all people, believers and unbelievers alike. Yet, pain and suffering need not be pointless or wasted. Suffering can be redemptive when accepted and offered up to God in sacrifice. God shows that He can use suffering for a divine good purpose.

He *[Jesus]* was not ashamed of the cross, for it was effecting the salvation of the world. Indeed, it was no common man who was suffering. It was God made man, striving for the prize of His endurance.

The Savior endured these things, and made peace through the blood of the cross for things in heaven and things on earth. We were enemies of God through sin, and God had appointed the sinner to die. It was necessary, then, that one of two things should happen: either that God, in His truth, should destroy all men, or that in His loving-kindness He should blot out the sentence. But behold the wisdom of God. He preserved both the truth of His sentence, and the exercise of His loving kindness. Christ bore our sins in His body on the tree, so that by His death we might die to sin and live to righteousness.

Saint Cyril of Jerusalem (AD 315–386), *Catechetical Lectures*, 13. 6, 33

Jesus meets the women of Jerusalem: Eighth Station of the Cross (Luke 23:27–31)—Only Luke notes the women who follow Jesus. According to the Talmud, Jews are forbidden to lament for anyone condemned to death. Yet, these women bewail and lament the suffering of the innocent Jesus. He says: *Daughters of Jerusalem, do not weep for me, but weep for yourselves and for your children. For behold, the days are coming when they will say, "Blessed are the barren, and the wombs that never bore, and the breasts that never nursed!"* (Luke 23:28–29). For a culture in which childbearing remains the greatest blessing from God, these words shock the women. Jesus again warns the women about the coming destruction of Jerusalem.

Luke does not mention any of the women by name, but the other evangelists name six or seven women who stood near the Cross. The third and fourth in this list may be one and the same person, and if so, there were three Mary's, not four:
+ Mary the mother of the Lord (John 19:25)
+ Mary Magdalene (Mark 15:40; Matthew 27:55; John 19:25)
+ Mary the mother of James and Joses (Mark 15:40; Matthew 27:55)
+ Mary the wife of Clopas (John 19:25)
+ Salome (Mark 15:40)
+ The mother of James and John (Matthew 27:55)
+ The sister of the Lord's mother (John 19:25).

Green wood refers to young, life-giving sprouts. Jesus is the young, innocent, life-giving One. Dry wood is dead and only good for burning up in the fire. Dry wood represents unrepentant, unbelieving people (Luke 23:31).

Jesus is stripped of His garments: Tenth Station of the Cross (Luke 23:34b)—Jews abhor any form of public nudity. Pious Jews would have modestly turned their gaze away from the nakedness of Jesus on the Cross. The Passion narratives discreetly avoid describing how He was stripped, and they only say that while He hung from the Cross the soldiers divided His garments. The Romans had no scruples about handling bloody clothes on a high holy day, as Jews did. Hebrew onlookers might remember the coat of many colors that had been stripped from Joseph and smeared with goat's blood (Genesis 37:31). Only because Jesus lost His fine robe do we learn that in life He had worn an exceptional, seamless, outer garment.

Jesus is nailed to the Cross: Eleventh Station of the Cross (Luke 23:32–43)—Criminals were usually tied to a cross and hung for days, dying from dehydration. No longer able to support the body weight, the chest would collapse, causing suffocation. Due to the onset of the Sabbath, Jesus had to die more quickly, and so nails were used, causing more blood loss and accelerating death. None of the evangelists mentions the nails, but the risen Jesus later invites doubting Thomas to touch the nail marks in His hands (John 20:27). Nails were pounded in the wrist between the radius and ulna bones. Spikes were driven into the feet, and there may have been a slight footrest to keep the body erect. The Psalmist foretold: *they have pierced my hands and feet—I can count all my bones—they stare and gloat over me* (Psalm 22:16–17). Some crucifixes show nails piercing the center of the palms, but there they could not have supported His weight. Other crucifixes correctly show the nails piercing the wrist. The Shroud of Turin depicts the wound images on the wrists.

Despite Jesus' pain, dehydration, and weakened conditioned as He hung dying upon the Cross, He managed to utter a few sentences known as the "Seven Last Words." Two are quotations from the Book of Psalms (Psalms 22:1; 31:5), revealing that Jesus prayed or at least tried to pray the entire psalm. *Father, into your hands I commit my spirit!* (Luke 23:46) reflects a psalm that Jesus may have prayed with Mary and Joseph as a child. *Into your hand I commit my spirit; you have redeemed me, O Lord, faithful God* (Psalm 31:5) shows complete faith in a loving Father, who can redeem impossible situations and even raise the dead to life.

Seven Last Words of Christ

Father, forgive them; for they know not what they do (Luke 23:34).
Truly, I say to you, today you will be with me in Paradise (Luke 23:43).
Woman, behold, your son! . . . Behold, your mother (John 19:26–27).
My God, my God, why have you forsaken me? (Matthew 27:46).
I thirst (John 19:28).
It is finished (John 19:30).
Father, into your hands I commit my spirit! (Luke 23:46).

Forgiveness—Only Luke reports Jesus' words of mercy from the Cross: *Father, forgive them; for they know not what they do* (Luke 23:34). Peter recalls the words of Our Lord when he says, *You . . . killed the Author of life, whom God raised from the dead. . . . And now, brethren, I know that you acted in ignorance, as did also your rulers* (Acts

3:14–15, 17). Stephen must also have remembered Jesus' words, when he said, *Lord, do not hold this sin against them* (Acts 7:60). Jesus, who came to call sinners to repentance, continues to show divine mercy to sinners.

Despite scoffing and mocking, several truths emerge inadvertently. Truthfully, Jesus is *the Christ of God, his Chosen One! . . . The King of the Jews* (Luke 23:35, 37, 38). Luke contrasts the common people, *laos* in Greek, who stand by watching Jesus, and the religious leaders and soldiers who taunt and mock Him. Some of the common people accompany Jesus to comfort Him.

The good thief, called Saint Dismas in the Orthodox Church, knows that he is a sinner deserving of punishment, and he repents. He does everything necessary for conversion and salvation. The good thief acknowledges his sin, believes in Jesus, and asks for mercy. This repentant sinner expresses faith that Jesus is a king and has the authority to pardon sinful criminals. Jesus speaks some of the most hopeful words in the Bible: *Truly, I say to you, today you will be with me in Paradise* (Luke 23:43). Dismas only asked that Jesus remember him, but Jesus always gives more than anyone can ask or imagine. Jesus gives eternal life in His Kingdom—heaven. Even a thief might steal a place in heaven, if he repents of his sin and believes in Jesus. In human courts, confessing to a crime results in punishment and prison. Whereas, confessing one's sins to God results in freedom and redemption.

The two thieves on the crosses illustrate two aspects of divine providence. Free will and grace are given to every person. Both thieves are in the same place. They are both guilty sinners. They both gaze into the face of pure love and divine mercy. One thief clings to his hardened heart, freely choosing to mock and blaspheme Jesus. He refuses to repent and receive mercy. The other thief chooses to embrace the grace that is offered, the grace of repentance. The good thief repents, prays, and is promised a place in the kingdom of God. The same choices are given to all people today.

Jesus dies on the Cross: Twelfth Station of the Cross (Luke 23:44–49)—*It was now about the sixth hour, and there was darkness over the whole land until the ninth hour, while the sun's light failed; and the curtain of the temple was torn in two* (Luke 23:44–45). The prophet Joel predicted that the sun would turn to darkness on the great and awesome day of the Lord (Joel 2:31). Amos foretold the same ominous sign; *"And on that day," says the Lord GOD, "I will make the sun go down at noon, and darken the earth in broad daylight"* (Amos 8:9). Even secular historians of antiquity report the darkness over the land and the tearing of the thick temple curtain.

For Luke, the death of Jesus is the moment when He sends His Spirit to the Father. The psalmist consigned only his own human soul to the Father in this verse (Psalm 31:5), but Jesus also means the return of the divine Spirit. Thus all three Persons of the Blessed Trinity are contained in the last of the seven words. Luke, of course, will tell how the divine Spirit returns in the Pentecost event (Acts 2).

It is customary, in making the Stations of the Cross, for the participants to kneel for a moment of silence upon reaching the Twelfth Station, at the death of Jesus, as the sun was darkened and the curtain of the temple was torn in two. Matthew and Mark mention that the curtain was torn in two from top to bottom (Matthew 27:51; Mark 15:38). That was the same veil behind which the Archangel Gabriel had appeared to Zechariah as Luke's Gospel began (Luke 1:11).

> This veil, at the very moment of Jesus' death, is torn in two from top to bottom. There are two things we learn from this: on the one hand, it becomes apparent that the era of the old Temple and its sacrifices is over. In place of symbols and rituals that point ahead to the future, the reality has now come, the crucified Jesus who reconciles us all with the Father. At the same time, though, the tearing of the Temple veil means that the pathway to God is now open. Previously God's face had been concealed. Only in a symbolic way could the high priest once a year enter his presence. Now God himself has removed the veil and revealed himself in the crucified Jesus as the one who loves to the point of death. The pathway to God is open.
>
> Pope Emeritus Benedict XVI, *Jesus of Nazareth, II*
> (San Francisco: Ignatius Press, 2011), 209

Thus, the tearing of the temple curtain, which separated the common people from God, signifies the close of the Old Covenant and the beginning of the New Covenant. Through the precious blood of Jesus, shed upon the Cross, all people now have access to God. Christ freely gave up His life to atone for the sins of the world and reconcile all of humanity with the Father. Anyone who repents and believes in Jesus can now have a personal relationship with God.

Jesus is taken down from the Cross: Thirteenth Station (Luke 23:49–53)—*Now there was a man named Joseph from the Jewish town of Arimathea. He was a member of the council, a good and righteous man, who had not consented to their purpose and deed, and he was looking for the kingdom of God* (Luke 23:50–51). All four Gospels tell how Joseph of Arimathea took charge of the arrangements for Jesus' body. Mark says that he *took courage* (Mark 15:43) to approach Pilate after the death of Jesus to obtain the body. Joseph risks rejection and shunning by other members of the Sanhedrin when they learn what he has done. Only John mentions that the Pharisee Nicodemus also came, bringing a mixture of myrrh and aloes to preserve the body of Jesus within the shroud (John 19:39).

The body of Jesus is laid in the tomb: Fourteenth Station (Luke 23:53–56)—At that time, Calvary stood outside the city walls. It was forbidden to execute or to bury anyone within the walls. Joseph of Arimathea had a new tomb hewn out in a garden (John 19:41), just a few paces from the place of crucifixion. Perhaps he had foreseen that some innocent man would need burial, and he would be able to do a good deed and bury the dead, as Tobit had done (Tobit 2:7). Most criminals were thrown into common graves. However,

Joseph provides Jesus with a proper burial, fit for a King. The Latin Church calls the tomb the *Sepulchre,* or tomb, but the Eastern Church calls it the *Anastasis,* or place of resurrection. When those who love Jesus place His horribly abused body in the tomb, they expect that it will rise again in the general resurrection on the last day. Jesus had talked about the "third day," but they had no idea what that meant. Soon they would find out, but for now, they grieve for Jesus, their teacher and friend—the fallen King.

Jesus has many lovers of His heavenly kingdom but few cross-bearers. Many desire His consolation, but few His tribulation. Many will sit down with Him at table, but few will share His fast. All desire to rejoice with Him, but few will suffer for Him.

Many will follow Him to the breaking of the bread, but few will drink the bitter cup of His Passion. Many revere His miracles, but few follow the shame of His cross. Many love Jesus when all goes well with them, and praise Him when He does them a favor; but if Jesus conceals Himself and leaves them for a little while, they fall to complaining and become depressed.

They who love Jesus purely for Himself and not for their own sake bless Him in all trouble and anguish as well as in time of consolation. Even if He never sent them consolation, they would still praise Him and give thanks.

Oh how powerful is the pure love of Jesus, when not mixed with self-interest or self-love! . . . Where will a person be found ready to serve God without looking for a reward? It is hard to find anyone so spiritual who is willing to be stripped of all things. Where will you find a person truly poor in spirit and free from all attachment to creatures? Such a one is a *rare treasure brought from distant shores* (Proverbs 31:14).

If we were to give up all our possessions, it is still nothing; if we did severe penance, it is but little; if we acquired all knowledge, still are we far from virtue. Even if we had great virtue and fervent devotion, we would still be lacking that one thing necessary above all else.

And what is that one thing? That leaving all things behind, we should leave self, renouncing our self completely and keeping nothing of self-love. And then when we have done all things that we know we ought to do, let us think that we have done nothing. . . . As our Lord, the Truth, has said: "When you have done all you have been commanded to do, say, 'We are useless servants'" (Luke 17:10). Then will we be truly poor in spirit and able to say with the Prophet: "I am alone and afflicted" (Psalms 25:16). Yet there is no one richer or more powerful, no one more free than we are, if we know how to renounce ourselves and all things, putting ourselves in the lowest place.

Thomas a Kempis, *The Imitation of Christ*
(New York: Catholic Book Pub. 1993), 89–90.

The Power of Christ's Blood

If we wish to understand the power of Christ's blood, we should go back to the ancient account of its prefiguration in Egypt. *Sacrifice a lamb without blemish,* commanded Moses, *and sprinkle its blood on your door.* If we were to ask him what he meant, and how the blood of an irrational beast could possibly save men endowed with reason, his answer would be that the saving power lies not in the blood itself, but in the fact that it is a sign of the Lord's blood. In those days, when the destroying angel saw the blood on the door he did not dare to enter, so **how much less will the devil approach now when he sees, not the figurative blood on the doors, but the true blood on the lips of believers,** the doors of the temple of Christ.

If you desire further proof of the power of this blood, remember where it came from, how it ran down from the cross, flowing from the Master's side. The gospel records that when Christ was dead, but still hung on the cross, a soldier came and pierced His side with a lance and immediately there poured out water and blood. Now water was a symbol of baptism and the blood, of the Holy Eucharist. The soldier pierced the Lord's side, he breached the wall of the sacred temple, and I have found the treasure and made it my own. . . .

Beloved, do not pass over this mystery without thought; it has yet another hidden meaning, which I will explain to you. I said that water and blood symbolized baptism and the Holy Eucharist. From these two sacraments the Church is born: from baptism, *the cleansing water that gives rebirth and renewal through the Holy Spirit,* and from the Holy Eucharist. Since the symbols of baptism and the Eucharist flowed from His side, it was from His side that Christ fashioned the Church, as He had fashioned Eve from the side of Adam.

Moses gives a hint of this when he tells the story of the first man and makes him exclaim: *Bone from my bones and flesh from my flesh!* As God then took a rib from Adam's side to fashion a woman, so Christ has given us blood and water from His side to fashion the Church. God took the rib when Adam was in a deep sleep, and in the same way Christ gave us the blood and water after His own death.

Do you understand, then, how Christ has united His bride to Himself and what food He gives us all to eat? By one and the same food we are both brought into being and nourished. As a woman nourishes her child with her own blood and milk, so does Christ unceasingly nourish with His own blood those to whom He Himself has given life.

Saint John Chrysostom, bishop (AD 347–407),
Catechesis, 3, 13–19

1. Explain the complaints made against Jesus.

Luke 23:1–2
Luke 23:5
Mark 15:3

2. What did Pilate ask Jesus? What was Pilate's conclusion?

Luke 23:3
John 18:38
Luke 23:4
Luke 23:14
Luke 23:22

3. Who is responsible for condemning Jesus?

Luke 23:1–21
CCC 591
CCC 596–598

* Are we guilty of the death of Jesus?

4. Describe Barabbas. Luke 23:18–19, 25

5. Who helped Jesus? How did he help? Luke 23:26

* Share some ways in which other Christians have helped you.

6. Describe the scenario below.

Luke 23:27	
Luke 23:28	
Luke 23:29	
Luke 23:30	

7. How did Jesus forewarn people of calamity in Jerusalem? Luke 21:20–24

** What will the daughters (and sons) of Jerusalem experience in AD 70?

8. Describe the way in which Jesus would die. Luke 23:32–33

9. Explain the reaction of different groups of people to Jesus' suffering.

Luke 23:35a—*people*
Luke 23:35b—*rulers*
Luke 23:36ff—*soldiers*
Luke 23:39—*criminal*
Luke 23:40ff—*second criminal*

10. What does the thief ask? What does Jesus give? What does this reveal to you?

Luke 23:42
Luke 23:43
Luke 23:34
CCC 2616

* What hope can you find in the passages above?

11–12. Find the fulfillment of Old Testament prophecies below.

Psalm 22:18
Luke 23:34b
Psalm 69:21
Luke 23:36
Amos 8:9
Luke 23:44–45

13. What happened in the temple when Jesus died? Luke 23:45b

14. To whom does Jesus commend His life?

Psalm 31:5
Luke 23:46
CCC 730

15. Describe the people who have faith in Jesus' divinity. Luke 23:47–49

16–17. List and meditate on the Seven Last Words of Christ.

Luke 23:34
Luke 23:43
John 19:26–27
Matthew 27:46
John 19:28
John 19:30
Luke 23:46

18. Who was Joseph of Arimathea? Luke 23:50–51

19. What kindness did Joseph of Arimathea show to Jesus? Luke 23:52–53

20. What did the women do? Luke 23:55–56

* What practical kindness could you show to Jesus today?

CHAPTER 21

Risen Indeed
Luke 24

The Lord has risen indeed, and has appeared to Simon!
Luke 24:34

Matthew and Mark (even in the longer form) have relatively short Resurrection accounts, only up to twenty verses. It is as if they got writer's block before the challenge of narrating what, after all, took place in an empty tomb before an audience comprised exclusively of angels. Luke and John take more time and convey more about the appearances of the Lord to the disciples. Luke has fifty verses in the last chapter of his Gospel and John has fifty-six verses in his last two chapters.

The first Easter morning—*But on the first day of the week, at early dawn, they went to the tomb, taking the spices which they had prepared* (Luke 24:1). At dawn, Jews throughout the world looked toward the rising sun to give thanks to God for the gift of another day added to one's lifetime. The rising of the sun on the first day of the week was the occasion for the greatest thanks, because that is when God had said, *Let there be light* (Genesis 1:3) and had begun to create the world. All righteous Jews throughout the world were joined in special prayer on that Easter morning, which fell during the eight days of the Passover celebration. Their prayers would be answered more magnificently than they could ever have imagined.

At first dawn, one woman (in John's Gospel), two women (in Matthew), three women (in Mark), and five or more women (in Luke) approach the tomb. They walk through the streets, their footfalls echoing against the stones, arriving when the world is still half dark, but already half lit. Surprisingly, they see that the stone has been rolled back, and then are dazzled by the spectacle of two angels in bright apparel. Back in the first chapter of Luke's Gospel, the old priest Zechariah had sung of *the tender mercy of our God, when the day shall dawn upon us from on high to give light to those who sit in darkness and in the shadow of death* (Luke 1:78–79). That day has now dawned.

Assuming that the two bright angels speak separately rather than in unison, the first angel asks: *Why do you seek the living among the dead?* Then the second angel says, *Remember how he told you, while he was still in Galilee, that the Son of man must be delivered into the hands of sinful men, and be crucified, and on the third day rise* (Luke 24:5–7). Luke leaves implied the angelic commission: *Go quickly and tell his disciples that he has risen from the dead* (Matthew 28:7). Luke also leaves out the instruction for the Apostles to go to Galilee, because this evangelist limits his narrative to the events of Easter Day itself.

Now it was Mary Magdalene and Joanna and Mary the mother of James and the other women with them who told this to the apostles (Luke 24:10). The women of Good Friday were also the women of Easter Sunday. Luke does not name the women who were present at Calvary, but the other three evangelists do, and naturally the women who stood by the dying Jesus were the same women who returned to finish preparing His body. These women had more freedom of action than the men, because they would be less likely to be arrested for sedition. So the women become like angels to the men.

Salome is another woman in the garden, as mentioned by Mark (16:1). She is not, of course, the Salome who danced for the head of John the Baptist. Some suggest that this Salome was the mother of James the Greater and John, the sons of Zebedee. We don't know for sure, but Luke has room for this woman too in his well-populated garden.

Joanna, the second woman, appearing only in Luke's account, appears earlier in the same Gospel as the wife of Chuza, the steward of King Herod Antipas (Luke 8:3). She has already given alms to Jesus and his band during better days, and now she is probably the source for some of the funds for burial items needed on this occasion. Her name is the female form of the name John and Chuza means "the one who loves the Lord."

Mary, the mother of James the Lesser and Joses, is named in this group of women by Matthew, Mark, and Luke. Mary seems to have been a very popular name among Jewish women of the first century. It derives from the name of Moses' sister Miriam, but has mutated into Maryam, meaning "woman of sadness." The three Mary's were sorrowful women on Good Friday, but they became women of joy on Easter Sunday.

Mary Magdalene is known, in the Dominican tradition, as *apostola apostolorum*, "apostle to the apostles." The other women see angels, but Mary Magdalene sees more. John gives the fullest account of her activities on the first Easter—she finds the tomb empty, runs to tell Peter and the beloved disciple, and then returns to the tomb where she becomes the first person to see the risen Lord. Then, she returns to the disciples and tells them, *I have seen the Lord* (John 20:18). She had seen Him on Good Friday, and now she sees Him on Easter too. She tells the disciples what she knows and leaves it up to them whether to believe or not. They must have been swayed by her joy. Three days of grief, a pure grief, unmixed with the guilt of denial or betrayal, and now her mood had been completely transformed into joy. The guilty disciples, too, will have their grief transformed. They need to see firsthand so that they, in turn, will be able to testify to the world. But Mary Magdalene, because of her great love, has the privilege of being first to see, first to know, that the world had been changed forever. Her Master has brought to an end the reign of death; the darkness of the shadow of death no longer covers the earth.

Easter evening—*That very day two of them were going to a village named Emmaus, about seven miles from Jerusalem* (Luke 24:13). The longer version of the Marcan narrative has a brief summary of the Emmaus event. *After this he appeared in another form to two of them, as they were walking into the country* (Mark 16:12). Luke's version is much longer and occupies the whole middle section of his chapter.

Cle'opas is the name of one of the two disciples on the road to Emmaus. Luke does not report the name of the other one. Cle'opas is the masculine form of the Greek name Cleopatra. In Aramaic, these names can take the form Clopas and Clopatra. The Fourth Gospel includes someone named *Mary the wife of Clopas* among the women at the foot of the Cross (John 19:25). Thus it would seem possible that the wife Mary witnesses the Lord crucified, and her husband Cle'opas sees the Lord risen on the road to Emmaus.

Three fathers of the Church—Papias, Hegesippus, and Eusebius of Caesarea—pass on the information that Cle'opas was the brother of Joseph, the foster-father of Jesus, and that Cle'opas and Mary were the parents of Simeon, second bishop of Jerusalem. If this information is correct, then the third Mary at the foot of the Cross was the aunt of Jesus, and the man on the road to Emmaus was His uncle, who did not recognize Him because he appeared *in another form*, as Mark says.

Meeting someone unrecognized along the road is a familiar theme of Greek mythology. Oedipus met his father at a crossroads, failed to recognize him, and killed him. He thus became guilty of patricide, though ignorant of the fact. The gods sometimes came to earth and were mistreated by human passers-by, with bad consequences. Part of the beauty of the Emmaus account is how the seemingly chance encounter turns out so well. Jesus has been crucified in Jerusalem, but is appreciated on the road to Emmaus.

Eucharist at Emmaus—Since the Emmaus supper began at nightfall, it is already the next day, Monday, by the time Cle'opas and his companion recognized the Lord in the breaking of the bread. Remember that "breaking of bread" is Lucan language for the Eucharistic celebration. So the chance encounter on the road becomes a Eucharistic encounter. Thus the Lucan account of the death and Resurrection of Christ is framed by two liturgies—the Last Supper and the Supper at Emmaus. They are, in fact, one liturgy, offered by one and the same Celebrant.

> The Lord Jesus wanted those whose eyes were held lest they should recognize Him, to recognize Him in the breaking of the bread. The faithful know what I am saying. They know Christ in the breaking of the bread. For not all bread, but only that which receives the blessing of Christ, becomes Christ's body.
>
> Saint Augustine of Hippo (AD 354–430), *Sermons*, 234, 2

Holy Communion is the food for our pilgrimage, as it was for Cle'opas. At the Last Supper the disciples received the Body and Blood of Jesus living, because He had not yet suffered and died. At the Emmaus supper they received the Body and Blood of Jesus alive, because He is no longer dead. There was no liturgy during the hours that He was in the state of death. The liturgy of the Mass is one and the same sacrifice as Calvary, but the communicant receives the living Christ, not the corpse. Jesus lives now, and death has no more power over Him, and so His Eucharist is a gift of living flesh for eternal life.

Did not our hearts burn within us while he talked to us on the road, while he opened to us the Scriptures? (Luke 24:32). Jesus fed the hearts and minds of the disciples with the Liturgy of the Word before He fed their souls and bodies with the Liturgy of the Eucharist. Thus the Emmaus account contains a complete liturgy, both of word and of sacrament. The hearts of the disciples burned within them as He opened to them the Scriptures, because they hungered for the Scriptures to be explained to them. They were blessed first because they hungered (Luke 6:21), and secondly because the word was given and explained to them (Luke 24:27).

And they rose that same hour and returned to Jerusalem; and they found the Eleven gathered together and those who were with them (Luke 24:33). To the eleven Apostles, Cle'opas and his companion brought news—no longer first news, but not yet old news. They found the eleven in a state of agitation, because they had already heard reports of the Resurrection: *The Lord has risen indeed, and has appeared to Simon!* (Luke 24:34). When Jesus appeared to Peter, Easter moved from the realm of private to public revelation, though the event is told only in flashback. Luke does not say where the eleven were gathered, but it was probably the same upper room. The contract to use it probably applied to the whole fifty-day period from Passover to Pentecost, because distant pilgrims tended to stay for both feasts.

Then he led them out as far as Bethany, and lifting up his hands he blessed them (Luke 24:50). The last few verses of the Gospel jump forwards from Easter Sunday to forty days later (Acts 1:3). During that time, the risen Jesus appeared to more than five hundred disciples (1 Corinthians 15:6), adding up to a *cloud of witnesses* (Hebrews 12:1). After forty days, Jesus ascends into heaven. Luke describes the Ascension twice, once briefly at the end of his Gospel and again more fully at the beginning of Acts. Before Jesus ascends into heaven, He commissions His Apostles to *be my witnesses in Jerusalem and in all Judea and Samaria and to the end of the earth* (Acts 1:8). By the end of the Acts of the Apostles, Luke and Paul wind up in Rome, en route to Spain, which Jews at that time considered to be the end of the earth. Someone suggested that the subtitle of the two-part work Luke-Acts should be called "From Jerusalem to Rome," because the Gospel begins inside the Temple of Jerusalem and Acts ends with Paul preaching in Rome. The final commission by Jesus authorizes the Church to act throughout that whole territory.

The Apostles will not be able to fulfill their commission without the help of the Spirit, and so Jesus says to them, *And behold, I send the promise of my Father upon you; but stay in the city, until you are clothed with power from on high* (Luke 24:49). Jesus is talking about the Holy Spirit without actually using the name; rather, He uses the phrases *promise of my Father* and *power from on high*. Zechariah had spoken of *dawn upon us from on high*, and that was fulfilled on Easter morning. Jesus speaks of *power from on high,* and that will be fulfilled on Pentecost morning.

At the beginning of his Gospel, Luke promised to write an orderly account of events, and he does so by placing his Resurrection narrative in the exact center of his two-part work Luke-Acts. Everything in the Gospel leads up to the Resurrection, not as an end but as a climax. The entire book of Acts is a continuation of the Easter narrative. The risen Jesus continues to appear to the twelve Apostles into the first chapter and returns to appear to Saul on the road to Damascus (Acts 9:4ff). Jesus' appearance to Saul, central to all the Lucan and Pauline writings, is in fact an extension of the Resurrection narrative. Luke the researcher had the opportunity to interview a number of the people who saw the Lord risen, including Paul, his traveling companion for over a decade.

The Resurrection of Jesus continues to be the ethos of every action of all the Apostles, the focus of all their preaching. The Apostles are Easter people, eye-witnesses of the Risen Christ, willing to put their lives on the line for the One who has promised them a share in His eternal life. In Acts, Luke allows the Apostles to speak in their own authentic voices, as some do elsewhere in their own letters.

> Peter urged his fellow Apostles to elect a successor to Judas, someone to *become with us a witness to his resurrection* (Acts 1:22).
> The deacon Stephen declared, *I see the heavens opened, and the Son of man standing at the right hand of God* (Acts 7:56).
> Peter preached on Pentecost, *This Jesus God raised up, and of that we are witnesses* (Acts 2:32).
> Peter and John were apprehended *because they were teaching the people and proclaiming in Jesus the resurrection from the dead* (Acts 4:2).
> In the first years of Christianity, *with great power the apostles gave their testimony to the resurrection of the Lord Jesus, and great grace was upon them all* (Acts 4:33).
> Saul of Tarsus had his own vision of the risen Lord on the road to Damascus, told twice in Acts of the Apostles (Acts 9:3–7 and with additional details in 26:13–18).
> Paul *preached Jesus and the resurrection* everywhere—in Athens (17:18, 32), Jerusalem (23:6), Caesarea (24:15, 21), and even in Rome (28:30).

In Luke's Gospel, the Apostles came only slowly to the meaning of the Resurrection, but in the Acts of the Apostles, everything they do is suffused with this faith. The Resurrection of the Lord is the climax of the double book Luke-Acts; it is not an end but a beginning, for them and for all of us saved by Our Lord. We too are Easter people called to action. We too have testimony to offer to the new hope given the human race, by the rising of Jesus Christ from the dead. We must live in such a way as to leave no doubt that, where death once reigned, life is now triumphant. We say so by our words and, even more, by our actions.

God Has Made You Wise

I give glory to Jesus Christ, the God who has made you wise; for I have observed that you are set in faith unshakable, as if nailed to the cross of our Lord Jesus Christ in body and in soul; and that you are confirmed in love by the Blood of Christ, firmly believing in regard to our Lord that He is truly of the family of David according to the flesh, and God's Son by the will and power of God, truly born of a Virgin, baptized by John so that all justice might be fulfilled by Him, in the time of Pontius Pilate and Herod the Tetrarch truly nailed in the flesh on our behalf—and we are the fruit of His divinely blessed passion—so that by means of His Resurrection He might raise aloft a banner for His saints and believers in every age, whether among the Jews or among the Gentiles, united in a single body in His Church.

He underwent all these sufferings for us, so that we might be saved; and He truly suffered, just as He truly raised Himself, not as some unbelievers contend, when they say that His passion was merely in appearance . . . I know and believe that He was in the flesh even after the Resurrection. And when He came to those with Peter, He said to them: "Here, now, touch Me, and see that I am not a bodiless ghost." Immediately, they touched Him and, because of the merging of His flesh and spirit, they believed. For the same reason they despised death, and in fact were proven superior to death. After His Resurrection He ate and drank with them, as a being of flesh, although He was united in spirit to the Father.

Saint Ignatius of Antioch (AD 100),
Letter to the Smyrnaeans, 1.1,2

1. What is significant about the day of the week?

Luke 24:1
CCC 2174
CCC 1166–1167

* What practical things do you do to make Sunday, the Lord's Day, special?

2. Who went to the tomb?

Luke 23:55–24:2
Luke 24:10a
Luke 24:10b

3. Explain the drama in the scenario below.

Luke 24:1–3
Luke 24:4–5
Luke 24:6–7
Luke 24:8–10

4. How did the disciples react to the words of the women?

Luke 24:11
Luke 24:12
CCC 641

5. What is necessary to believe in the Resurrection? CCC 648

6. What can you learn about the Resurrection? Is it an historical event?

Luke 24:5b
CCC 643
CCC 652
CCC 653
CCC 654
CCC 655

* How do you celebrate Easter, the supreme feast of the Catholic liturgical year?

7. Find another explanation for the empty tomb. Matthew 28:11–15

8. Where were the disciples supposed to be?

Matthew 26:32
Matthew 28:7
Mark 14:28; 16:7

9. Describe the drama on the Road to Emmaus.

Luke 24:13–14	
Luke 24:15–16	
Luke 24:17–18	
Luke 24:19–21	
Luke 24:22–24	
Luke 24:25–27	

10. Why didn't the disciples recognize Jesus? CCC 646

11. What do the disciples ask Jesus and why? Luke 24:28–29, 32

12. What does Jesus do at table? What does this recall? Find three common verbs.

Luke 24:30	
Luke 9:16	
Luke 22:19	

13. Explain the significance of this event.

CCC 645
CCC 1324
CCC 1329

14. What did the disciples from Emmaus do? Luke 24:33–34

* How and when can you share what God has done for you?

15. How do the disciples react when they see the risen Lord? Luke 24:36–37

16. What does Jesus invite the disciples to do? Why is this significant?

Luke 24:38–40
John 20:27
1 John 1:1

* Did Jesus allow His friends to touch Him?

17. What evidence can you find that Jesus was real, not a ghost?

Luke 24:41–43
John 21:10–13
Matthew 28:9

18. What did Jesus help the disciples to understand? Luke 24:44–47

19. Define the word "witness." How should a disciple witness? Matthew 28:19–20

20. What final promise and event is recorded? Where does Luke's Gospel end?

Luke 24:49
Luke 24:50–51
Luke 24:52

* How has the Lord spoken to you in your study of the Gospel of Luke?

Return to Galilee

To return to Galilee means *to re-read* everything on the basis of the cross and its victory, fearlessly: "do not be afraid." To re-read everything—Jesus' preaching, his miracles, the new community, the excitement and the defections, even the betrayal—to re-read everything starting from the end, which is a new beginning, *from this supreme act of love.*

For each of us, too, there is a "Galilee" at the origin of our journey with Jesus. "To go to Galilee" means something beautiful, it means rediscovering our baptism as a living fountainhead, drawing new energy from the sources of our faith and our Christian experience. To return to Galilee means above all to return to that blazing light with which God's grace touched me at the start of the journey. From that flame I can light a fire for today and every day, and bring heat and light to my brothers and sisters. That flame ignites a humble joy, a joy which sorrow and distress cannot dismay, a good, gentle joy.

In the life of every Christian, after baptism there is also another "Galilee," *a more existential "Galilee"*: the experience of a *personal encounter with Jesus Christ* who called me to follow him and to share in his mission. In this sense, returning to Galilee means treasuring in my heart the living memory of that call, when Jesus passed my way, gazed at me with mercy and asked me to follow him. To return there means reviving the memory of that moment when his eyes met mine, the moment when he made me realize that he loved me.. . . .

Each of us can ask: *What is my Galilee?* I need to remind myself, to go back and remember. *Where is my Galilee?* Do I remember it? Have I forgotten it? Seek and you will find it! There the Lord is waiting for you. Have I gone off on roads and paths which made me forget it? Lord, help me: tell me what my Galilee is; for you know that I want to return there to encounter you and to let myself be embraced by your mercy. Do not be afraid, do not fear, return to Galilee!

The Gospel is very clear: we need to go back there, to see Jesus risen, and to become witnesses of his resurrection. This is not to go back in time; it is not a kind of nostalgia. It is returning to our first love, in order to *receive the fire* which Jesus has kindled in the world and to bring that fire to all people, to the very ends of the earth. Go back to Galilee, without fear!

Pope Francis, *Easter Vigil Homily,* April 19, 2014

~ Study the entire Catholic Bible ~

Catholic Bible Study

- Commentaries by world-renowned Catholic biblical scholars
- Suitable for a large parish Bible Study or for a small home group
- Children's Bible Study books for pre-school children
- DVD lectures available for each study

About Our Authors

Bishop Jan Liesen, SSD—studied at the Pontifical Biblical Institute in Rome, writing his dissertation on the book of Sirach. He was a distinguished member of the Papal Theological Commission and is the Bishop of Breda in the Netherlands. Bishop Liesen is the primary author of *Wisdom* and *The Gospel of Mark*.

Father Joseph Ponessa, SSD—earned a doctorate in Sacred Scripture at the the Biblicum. He is the primary author of *The Gospels of John and Luke, Genesis, Moses and the Torah, Acts and Letters, David and the Psalms, Prophets and Apostles, Return from Exile,* and *The Rise and Fall of Ancient Israel.*

Monsignor Charles Kosanke, STD—studied at the Pontifical Gregorian University in Rome, taught at Sacred Heart Seminary, and was rector of Saints Cyril and Methodius Seminary in Michigan. He is the primary author of *Isaiah.*

Father Ponessa, Bishop Liesen, Monsignor Kosanke

Monsignor Jan Majernik, STD—a native of Slovakia, earned a doctorate in Sacred Scripture from the Franciscan School of Biblical Studies in Jerusalem. He studied biblical archeology and biblical languages at the Hebrew University in Israel and at the Biblicum in Rome. He is the primary author of *The Synoptics.*

Father Andreas Hoeck, SSD—born in Cologne, Germany and earned his doctorate at the Pontifical Biblical Institute in Rome, where he wrote his dissertation on the book of Revelation. He is the academic dean at Saint John Vianney Seminary in Denver and he is the author of *Ezekiel, Hebrews, Revelation.*

Laurie Manhardt

Laurie Watson Manhardt, PhD—earned a doctorate in education from the University of Michigan. She writes all of the home study questions and the children's books. Laurie wrote the commentaries on *Leviticus, Numbers, Psalms, Proverbs, Ecclesiastes, Wisdom, Judith, Esther, Romans, Philippians, Galatians, 1 and 2 Timothy, Titus,* and *1 and 2 Peter.*

Sharon Doran, MA—earned a Master's in Pastoral Theology with an emphasis in Sacred Scripture from the Augustine Institute in Denver. She founded the Seeking Truth Catholic Bible Study in Omaha and wrote *Judges, Amos, and Hosea.* Sharon and her husband Steve have five sons.

Sharon Doran

Sr. Margarita Gómez, RMI—a Claretian sister born in Spain, completed her S.T.L. at the Pontifical Gregorian University, Rome, and teaches Sacred Scripture at Saint John Vianney Seminary in Boynton Beach, FL. Sister translates our books into Spanish.

Basic, Foundational Books

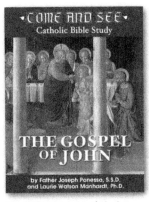

The Gospel of John — This perfect starting place covers the life of Jesus and the sacraments of Baptism, Holy Eucharist, Matrimony and Holy Orders in 21 lessons. *202 pages*

El Evangelio según San Juan — Este texto es el que mejor presenta la vida de Jesus y los Sacramentos de la Eucaristia, el Matrimonio y el Orden en 21 lecciones. *202 pages*

Genesis — Looks at creation through the lens of science, and the lives of Adam and Eve, Noah, Abraham, Isaac and Jacob, in this 22 chapter study. *216 pages*

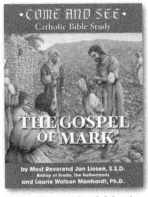

The Gospel of Mark — Delve into the oldest gospel on record. Mark's Gospel recounts the life, ministry and miracles of Jesus of Nazareth in this 18 week study. *220 pages*

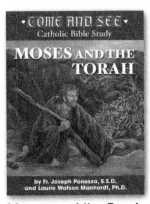

Moses and the Torah — Complete the Pentateuch: *Exodus, Leviticus, Numbers,* and *Deuteronomy* in this 22 week study, as Moses brings God's law to the people. *220 pages*

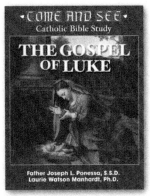

The Gospel of Luke—This 21 week study begins with the infancy narratives and early life of Jesus and continues to the Ascension of Our Lord. *220 pages*

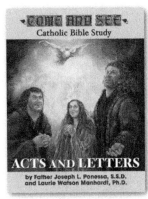

Acts and Letters — Explore the early Church through Saint Luke's writing on the *Acts of the Apostles* and the letters of Saint Paul to Christian communities in this 22 week New Testament study. *220 pages*

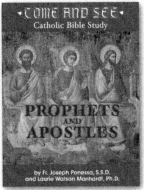

Prophets and Apostles — See how the Old Testament prophets looked forward to God's promised Messiah while the New Testament apostles find fulfillment of prophecy in the life of Jesus. *206 pages*

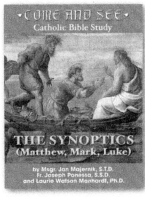

The Synoptics — Compare *Matthew, Mark,* and *Luke's* accounts of the life of Jesus as you journey through the Holy Land in this 22 week overview of the Gospels. *204 pages*

Advanced, Challenging Books

David and the Psalms— This 22 week study examines the lives of Ruth, Samuel and David, and their prayers which emerge in the life of Christ and echo in His Church, from the books of *Ruth, 1 and 2 Samuel* and *Psalms. 208 pages*

Isaiah — This major Old Testament prophet's writings have been called the fifth Gospel because his prophecies point to Jesus of Nazareth, the Suffering Servant and Redeemer of the world. This is a 22 chapter study. *214 pages*

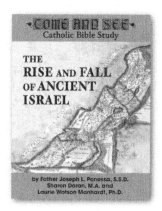

The Rise and Fall of Ancient Israel — Learn about the history of ancient Israel with this extensive 21 week study of historical books and prophets: *Joshua, Judges, 1 and 2 Kings, 1 and 2 Chronicles, Amos, Hosea,* and *Jeremiah. 220 pages*

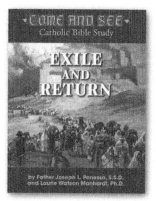

Exile and Return — In this 22 week Bible Study, the books of *Tobit, Judith, Esther, Ezra, Nehemiah,* and *1 and 2 Maccabees* show ways in which God worked in the lives of the Jewish people as they returned from their exile in Babylon to the Holy Land. *220 pages*

Wisdom—In this 22 chapter study, Bishop Liesen provides marvelous commentary on the Wisdom literature of the Bible, studying *Job, Proverbs, Ecclesiastes, Song of Solomon (Song of Songs), Wisdom,* and *Sirach. 220 pages*

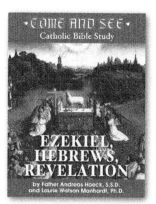

Ezekiel, Hebrews, Revelation —The Prophet Ezekiel experiences amazing visions similar to those of the Apostle John revealed in the book of *Revelation. The Letter to the Hebrews* reveals Jesus the High Priest in this 22 lesson study. *220 pages*

www.CatholicBibleStudy.net   (772) 321-4034

www.EmmausRoad.org   (800) 398-5470   (740) 283-2880

Come and See KIDS Books

Come and See KIDS is a Bible Study series written for pre-school to early elementary school age children. These companion books to the adult series could also be used alone.

- Bible memory verses and a Bible story
- Coloring pages illustrating the Bible story
- Craft activities for the child to make with a little bit of help

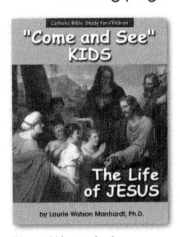

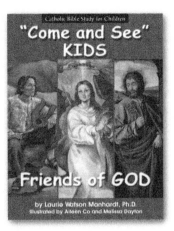

The Life of Jesus—Teaches about the life of Jesus with stories, prayers, coloring pages and crafts. 23 lessons cover the Annunciation to the Resurrection. *128 perforated pages*

In the Beginning—Goes with *Genesis* and teaches children about God's creation. 23 lessons include stories from creation through the story of Joseph and his brothers.

Friends of God—Can accompany any adult book. 22 lessons cover heroes of the Bible. Some children and young people from the Bible are: Samuel, David, Daniel, Mary the Mother of God, and the little boy who shared his lunch with Jesus.

⟶ Endorsements ⟵

"The *Come and See ~ Catholic Bible Study* series provides an in depth and detailed analysis of the books of the Bible and is both an educational and spiritual way of approaching the word of God as revealed in Sacred Scripture."
Most Reverend Gerald M. Barbarito,
Bishop of Palm Beach, FL

"We found this Bible Study to be unique in several ways. It required personal preparation, reading the chapter and its excellent commentary provided by the authors, and answering questions that connected the chapter with other passages in the Old and New Testament and in the *Catechism of the Catholic Church*. The questions also invited us to personal reflection and to apply the teachings to our personal lives and to the problems of today. Thus, we learned a lot!"
Dr. and Mrs. Renato Gadenz, Eatontown, NJ

"The *Come and See ~ Catholic Bible Studies* are excellent and are helping men and women all over the country better understand the Bible and its relationship to the Catholic Church… Highly recommended."

Ralph Martin, S.T.D.,
President, Renewal Ministries, Ann Arbor
Director, New Evangelization,
Sacred Heart Seminary, Detroit, MI

"Certainly this is THE BEST study on the market. Not just because it is the least expensive, no, but, because it is so well done. I've researched extensively. It IS the best. Our parish is in the 10th year of *Come and See ~ Catholic Bible Study* and loving it!"
Chris Snyder,
Marlborough, MA

Emmaus Road Publishing
1468 Parkview Circle
Steubenville, OH 43952

Come and See ~ Catholic Bible Study
www.CatholicBibleStudy.net
(772) 321-4034

Seeking Truth Bible Study
www.SeekingTruth.net

www.EmmausRoad.org   (800) 398-5470   (740) 283-2880

Prayer Requests

Prayer Requests

CPSIA information can be obtained
at www.ICGtesting.com
Printed in the USA
BVOW07s1723030916
461053BV00006B/8/P